Samuel Jonas

A selection of Psalms and hymns, done under appointment of the Philadelphian Association

Samuel Jonas

A selection of Psalms and hymns, done under appointment of the Philadelphian Association

ISBN/EAN: 9783337101961

Printed in Europe, USA, Canada, Australia, Japan

Cover: Foto ©Lupo / pixelio.de

More available books at **www.hansebooks.com**

SELECTION

OF

PSALMS AND HYMNS,

DONE UNDER THE APPOINTMENT

OF THE

PHILADELPHIAN ASSOCIATION.

By *SAMUEL JONES*, D. D.
AND
BURGIS ALLISON, A. M.

PHILADELPHIA:
PRINTED BY R. AITKEN & SON, AT
N°. 22. MARKET STREET;
M,DCC,XC.

PREFACE.

IT is thought the following notes may be sufficient.

1. The Psalms are all of Dr. Watts' version.
2. The Collection, referred to at the beginning of many of the following Hymns, is a collection of Psalms and Hymns of singular merit, but without a name, printed in London, 1774.
3. The most of those attributed to Cennick, Hart, Steele, Davis, Robinson, and Ken, were taken from the above collection, as also many of Dr. Watts' psalms and hymns; and those names, except Watts', annexed to them from Dr. Rippon. The other names were generally taken from collection of Rippon's, which is a valuable work.
4. The letters, J, and A, are the initials of the respective selecters, Jones and Allison.
5. It is not designed that those Hymns appointed to be sung at the opening of public worship, before sermon, and after sermon, should be invariably used on those occasions only, but every one is left to his own discretion.
6. Notwithstanding the Hymns in the latter part of the Book are principally designed for

private

private use, yet they may be used in public, in such Congregations as are gennerally acquainted with tunes suited to them.

7. This Collection is restricted to a small size, with a view to lessen the price, and to render it more portable. It is thought, however, that no material inconvenience will follow, except that sometimes it may be difficult to find an Hymn after sermon, that will accord with the subject of discourse: but the Hymns under the word Distinction, in the Index, which are of general import, will in a good degree remedy the defect.

8. By the Scheme of General Contents, wherein the Hymns on the different occasions are duly arranged, any Hymn wanted may be, in a general way, pretty readily found: Nevertheless, a Table of First Lines follows, as also an Index of more particular contents at the end of the Book.

S. JONES.

Lower-Dublin, October 1, 1790.

TABLE
OF FIRST LINES.

A.

	Hymn, &c.
A FORM of words tho' e'er so sound,	65
Ah! lovely appearance of death,	326
Ah! what can I do,	336
Alas! and did my Saviour bleed,	83
Alas! what hourly dangers rise,	89
All gracious God, thy people bless,	152
All ye that pass by,	261
Almighty God of truth and love,	107
Am I a soldier of the cross,	97
And is it yet, dear Lord, a doubt,	259
And must this body die,	228
And now, my soul, another year,	76
And will the Lord thus condescend,	108
Another six days work is done,	13
Arise my soul, my joyful pow'rs,	75
Arise, O King of grace, arise,	194
Assist us, Lord, thy name to praise,	56
Awake and sing the song,	163
Awake my soul, and with the sun,	244
Awake my soul in joyful lays,	16
Awake my soul, awake mine eyes,	254
Awake our drowsy souls,	276
Awake, sweet gratitude, and sing,	63
Awake, ye Saints, and lift your eyes,	84

Before

B.

BEFORE Jehovah's awful throne,	1
Before thy throne, eternal King,	208
Behold the morning sun,	237
Beset with snares on every hand,	129
Be with me Lord, where e'er I go,	154
Bless, O my soul, the living God,	15
Blest are the souls, that hear and know,	60
Blest is the man, who shuns the place,	99
Blest is the man, for ever blest,	132
Blow ye the trumpet, blow,	274
Bless, O my soul the living God,	15
Brethren, let us join to bless,	290
Broad is the way that leads to death,	146

C.

CHILDREN of the Heavenly King,	287
Christ and his cross is all our theme,	113
Christians in your several stations,	319
Come all harmonious tongues,	158
Come, dearest Lord, descend and dwell,	150
Come, descend, O heavenly Spirit,	305
(1) Come gracious Spirit, heavenly dove,	18
Come, holy Spirit, come,	22
Come holy Spirit heavenly dove,	31
Come hither all ye weary souls,	17
Come humble sinners, in whose breast,	66
Come in ye blessed of your God,	186
Come, let us join our chearful songs,	190
Come Lord, and warm each languid heart,	30
Come, O my soul, and sing,	183
Come sinners, saith the mighty God,	55

Come

TABLE.

Come found his praise abroad,	24
Come thou Almighty King,	263
Come thou font of every blessing,	304
Come we that love the Lord,	23
Come weary souls, with sin distress'd,	128
Come ye sinners, come to Jesus,	315
Come ye sinners, poor and wretched,	312
Curst be the man, for ever curst,	144

D.

DEAR Jesus here comes.	339
Death as a sleep or gentle dose,	233
Dismiss us with thy blessing, Lord,	151
Does it not grief and wonder move,	47
Do we not know that solemn word,	168
Dread Sov'reign, let my evening song,	235
Dress uniform the soldier wears,	81

E.

EARTH has detained me pris'ner long,	34
Encourag'd by thy word,	207
Ere I sleep for every favour,	294
Eternal power, whose high abode,	43
Eternal source of joys divine,	74
Eternal wisdom, thee we praise,	26

F.

FAR from my thoughts vain world begone,	53
Father, before we hence depart,	68
Father, I sing thy wond'rous grace,	36
Father, I stretch my hands to thee,	100

	Hymn, &c.
Father, (if thou my Father art,)	328
Father of mercies, bow thine ear,	204
Father of mercies, in thy word,	28
Father, we wait to feel thy grace,	179
Frequent the day of God returns,	10
From thee, my God, my joys shall rise,	80

G.

GIVE thanks to God most high,	270
Give to our God immortal praise,	42
Glory be to God on high,	291
Glory to God, who gave the word,	82
Glory to thee, my God, this night,	243
Go, preach my Gospel, saith the Lord,	199
God moves in a mysterious way,	79
God of all consolation take,	92
God of my salvation hear,	277
Gracious Lord, incline thine ear,	288
Grace! tis a charming sound,	160
Great former of this various frame,	45
Great Father of mankind,	195
Great God indulge my humble claim,	41
Great God of wonders, all thy ways,	329
Great God, the Heav'ns well order'd frame,	332
Great Ruler of the earth and skies,	212
Great was the day, the joy was great,	198

H.

HAIL, Alpha and Omega, hail,	249
Hail, thou once despised Jesus,	300
Hark, from the tombs a doleful sound,	225

Hark

                                            Hymn, &c.
Hark! my soul, it is the Lord,   284
Hark! the voice of love and mercy,   314
He comes he comes, the judge severe,   321
He dies, the Heavenly lover dies,   127
He is a God of sovereign love,   91
Hear me O Redeemer hear,   280
Here at thy table, Lord, we wait,   177
High in the Heav'ns, eternal God,   49
Hosannah to Jesus on High,   327
Hosannah to the Prince of Light,   64
Hosannah with a chearful sound,   248
How are thy glories here displayed,   180
How beautious are their feet,   203
How condescending and how kind,   178
How firm a foundation the saints of the
    Lord,   341
How happy is the Christian state,   121
How pleas'd and blest was I,   196
How oft have sin and Satan strove,   142
How sad our state by nature is,   101
How short and hasty is our life,   133

                   I.

I Long to behold him aray'd,   325
    I love thy charming name,   58
I'll praise my Maker with my breath,   331
I'm tir'd of visits, modes and forms,   298
In a world of sin and sorrow,   306
In sweet exalted strains,   273
In such a grave as this,   175
Israel in ancient days,   268
In vain Apollo's silver tongue,   69
Is this the kind return,   166
                                            Jesus,

J

Jesus, and shall it ever be,	172
Jesu, friend of sinners hear,	278
Jesus, let thy pitying eye,	279
Jesus mighty King in Zion,	302
Jesus my All to heav'n is gone,	143
Jesus, O word divinely sweet,	188
Jesu, Redeemer, Saviour, Lord,	102
Jesus, the eternal Son of God,	32
Jesus, we bow before thy feet,	192

K

Kingdom of God not in word, but in power	65
Kind is the speech of Christ our Lord,	137

L

LAMB of God, we fall before thee,	301
Let all our tongues be one,	182
Let all the earth their voices raise,	333
Let ev'ry mortal ear attend,	98
Let them neglect thy glory Lord,	9
Let thy devoted servant go,	201
Let us love, and sing, and wonder,	318
Light of those, whose dreary dwelling,	299
Long did my soul in Jesus' form,	140
Long have I sat beneath the sound,	115
Lo he comes in clouds descending,	310
Lo! he cometh countless trumpets,	311
Lo the Almighty King of glory,	309
Lord at thy table I behold,	176
Lord bless thy saints assembled here,	197
Lord hast thou suffer'd me to see,	239

Lord

TABLE.

Lord how divine our comforts are,	189
Lord how mysterious are thy ways,	153
Lord how shall wretched sinners dare,	210
Lord in the morning thou shalt hear,	3
Lord dismiss us with thy blessing,	313
Lord I am vile conceiv'd in sin,	257
Lord I would spread my sore distress,	104
Lord Jesus, when, when shall it be,	156
Lord look on all assembled here,	216
Lord thou wilt hear me when I pray,	238
Lord we come before thee now,	283
Lord what a feeble piece,	229
Lord what a wretched land is this,	251
Lord when I read the traytor's doom,	67
Lord when our raptur'd thoughts survey,	27
Lord when thou didst ascend on high,	51
Loud let the tuneful trumpet sound,	46

M

MINE eyes and my desire,	157
Mistaken souls that dream of heav'n,	106
Most righteous God, my doom I bear,	296
My drowsy powers why sleep ye so,	112
My God, how endless is thy love,	246
My God in whom are all the springs,	125
My God, my God, and must I die,	232
My God my life, my love,	258
My God, my King, thy various praise,	141
My God, my portion, and my love,	73
My Lord, how great's the favour,	281
My Saviour, my Almighty friend,	87
My Saviour's pierced side,	159

My

TABLE.

	Hymn, &c.
My soul come meditate the day,	224
My soul how lovely is the place.	37

N

Naked as from the earth we came,	96
Not all the blood of beasts,	162
Not all the nobles of the earth,	256
Not unto us but thee alone,	72
Now begin the Heavenly theme,	289
Now from the altar of our hearts,	242
Now from the roaring lion's rage,	185
Now in the heat of youthful blood,	149
Now keep me stedfast dearest Lord,	♥174
Now let our voices join,	161
Now Lord another of thy days,	240
Now Lord the heavenly seed is sown,	85
Now Lord thy blessing add,	167
Now may the God of peace and love,	71
Now may the Spirit holy fire,	1
Now to the Lord a noble song,	134
Now Christ again to me appears,	343

O

O Come let us join,	260
O dearest Lord, give me an heart,	120
Of all the joys we mortals know,	130
O! for a glance of heav'nly day,	147
O for an heart to love my God,	29
O for a thousand tongues to sing,	6
O my soul was form'd for woe,	119
Oft as the bell with solemn toll,	123
Oft I reflect upon thy grace,	90
Often I seek my God by night,	252

O Jesus,

	Hymn, &c.
O Jesus, our Lord.	262
O Jesu, Jesu, dearest Lord,	86
O Lord, our Lord. how wond'rous great,	40
Once more before we part,	165
Once more my soul the rising day,	247
Once more we come before our God.	2
O that my load of sin were gone,	103
O that the Lord would guide my ways,	57
O thou, whose tender mercies hears,	78
O what shall I do to retrieve,	322
Our Saviour alone,	337
Out of the deeps of long distress,	62

P

PLEAS'D we read in sacred story,	307
Praise to the Lord, who bows his ear,	211
Precious bible what a treasure,	317
Press'd my soul with future prospect,	303

R

REJOICE the Lord is King,	267
Remember, Lord, our mortal state,	227
Rich grace, free grace, most sweetly call'd	61
Repent and be baptis'd,	274
Rise my soul adore thy maker,	293
Rise my soul and stretch thy wings,	282

S

SALVATION is forever nigh,	126
Salvation to our God,	25
Saviour I do feel thy merit,	303

Saviour

TABLE.

Saviour visit thy plantation,	316
See, gracious God, before thy throne,	215
See how the mounting sun,	241
See how the willing converts trace,	173
Sinners obey the gospel word,	145
Shew pity Lord, O Lord forgive,	147
Sleep downy sleep come close mine eyes,	255
So let our lips and lives express,	52
Soon as I hear'd my father say,	111
Sprinkled with reconciling blood,	11
Stay thou insulted spirit stay,	155
Stretch'd on the cross the Saviour dies,	181
Sweet is the mem'ry of thy grace,	33

T

THAT doleful night before his death,	187
The church a garden is,	266
Thee we adore eternal name,	221
The God Jehovah reigns,	164
The God of Abraham praise,	264
The great Redeemer we adore,	171
The God of glory sends his summons forth,	340
The heavens declare thy glory Lord,	48
The king of saints how fair his face,	50
The Lord descending from above,	8
The Lord how fearful is his name,	250
The Lord how glorious is his face,	184
The Lord my shepherd and my guide,	217
The Lord of earth and sky,	265
The praise of Zion waits for thee,	12
The presence of thy grace impart,	200
The Saviour calls let every ear,	5

TABLE.

The sinner that by precious faith,	118
The souls that would to Jesus press,	94
The spacious firmament on high,	124
There is a land of pure delight,	70
This specious earth is all the Lord's,	131
Tho' troubles assail and dangers affright,	338
Thou art, O God, a spirit pure,	44
Thou God of glorious Majesty,	297
Thou only source of true delight,	7
Thy presence Saviour may I feel,	122
'Tis a point I long to know,	285
'Tis false thou vile accuser, go,	148
'Tis finish'd the Redeemer said,	295
Thus was the great Redeemer purg'd,	170
Thus saith the wisdom of the Lord,	54
To day God bids the faithful rest,	236
To praise the ever bounteous Lord,	219
To our Redeemer's glorious name,	88
To thee, my God, I hourly sigh.	93
To thee who reign'st supreme above,	213
To thine Almighty arm we owe,	208
T'was the commission of our Lord,	169

U

UPWARD I lift mine eyes,   269

V

VAIN are the hopes the sons of men, 117
Vain man, thy fond pursuits forbear, 222

W

WE are a garden wall'd around,   135
We needs must die, who banish'd lie, 234

We

TABLE.

	Hymn, &c.
We sing to thee whose wisdom form'd,	253
Well met dear friends in Jesus name,	206
Welcome sweet day of rest,	21
Welcome thou well belov'd of God.	330
What different pow'rs of grace and sin,	116
What good news the angels bring,	286
What heav'nly man, or lovely God,	193
What scenes of horror and of death,	223
What shall I render to my God,	35
What think ye of Christ is the test,	323
What various hind'rances we meet,	14
What wisdom, majesty and grace.	39
When all thy mercies O my God,	218
When Abra'm full of sacred awe,	214
When God reveal'd his gracious name,	105
When, gracious Lord, when shall it be,	138
When I can read my title clear,	95
When I survey the wond'rous cross,	191
When Joseph his brethren beheld,	324
When, O dear Jesus, when shall I,	245
When the fierce north wind,	342
When with my mind divinely press'd,	297
While o'er our guilty land, O Lord,	209
While with ceaseless course the sun,	291
Who hath our report believed,	320
Why did the nations join to slay,	110
Why do we mourn departed friends,	230
Why is my heart so far from thee,	109
Why, O my heart, these anxious cares,	139
Why should our mourning thoughts delight,	231
Why should we start and fear to die,	226
With all my pow'rs of heart and tongue,	136
With all thy pow'r, O Lord descend,	202

With

	Hymn, &c.
With chearful voice I sing,	272
With joy we meditate the grace,	114
With heart and lips unfeign'd,	59
With rev'rence let the saints draw near,	4
When blooming youth is snatch'd away,	220

Y

YE nations round the earth rejoice,	20
Ye servants of God,	334
Ye souls that are weak,	335
Ye trembling souls dismiss your fears,	38
Ye tribes of Adam join,	271
Yonder, amazing sight I see,	77

GENERAL

I. At Opening Public Worship,
       From Hymn 1 to the 25
II. Before Sermon,   26 — 59
III. After Sermon,   60 — 167
IV. Baptism,   168 — 175
V. The Lord's Supper,   176 — 193
VI. Constitution of Churches, 194 — 197
VII. Ordination,   198 — 203
VIII. Association of Churches, 204 — 207
IX. Fasts and Thanksgiving,   208 — 219
X. Funeral Occasions,   220 — 234
XI. Family Worship,   235 — 259
XII. For Private Use,
     Personal and social, ⎫
     Of uncommon metres,   ⎬ 260 — 342
     as follows;   ⎭
  1. Twice 5 & 11, Winwick, &c.   260 — 262
  2. Twice 6 & 4, thrice 6 & 4,
             Whitefield,   — 263
  3. Twice 6, 8, & 4,   ditto,   — 264
  4. Four 6, & twice 8, Lenox, &c. 265 — 276
  5. 7 & 6, 7 & 6, 7, 8, 7 & 6, Salisbury, 277 — 278
  6. 7 & 6, do. do. Yorkshire,   — 280
  7. 7 & 6, 7 & 6, thrice 7 & 6, Dartford, — 281
  8. Sevens, Hotham Plymouth,   282 — 291
  9. 8, & twice 6, Havant,   292 — 294
  10. Twice 8, & 6, do. Chatham,   294 — 297
  11. Twice 8 & 6, thrice 8 & 6,   — 298
  12. 8 & 7, ditto, Welsh,   299 — 308
  13. 8 & 7, 8 & 7, 4 or 8, or 12, & 7,
       Helonsley,   309 — 316
                    GENERAL

GENERAL CONTENTS.

14. 8 & 7, 8 & 7, twice 7,   317 — 318
15. Twice 8 & 7, ditto,   319 — 320
16. Five 8 & 7, Trumpet,   — 321
17. Eights, New Jerusalem,   322 — 327
18. Eights, Luther,   328 — 330
19. Eights, Greenfield,   331 — 333
20. Twice 10, & twice 11, as 149 pſ. 334 — 339
21. Four 10 & twice 11 as the old 50,   — 340
22. Elevens   — 341
23. Thrice 11 & 5, Bunker-Hill,   — 342

A SELECTION

A SELECTION OF SALMS AND HYMNS, &c.

HYMN I. Common Metre. *J.*
Invoking the Spirit.

NOW may the Spirit's holy fire,
   Descending from above,
His waiting family inspire
   With joy, and peace, and love!

Thee we the Comforter confess;
   Unless thou'rt present here,
Our songs of praise are vain address,
   We utter heartless pray'r.

Wake, heav'nly Wind, arise, and come,
   Blow on the drooping field;
Our spices then shall breathe perfume,
   And fragrant incense yield.

Touch with a living coal the lip
   That shall proclaim thy word;
And bid each awful hearer keep
   Attention to the Lord.

A HYMN

HYMN II. Common Metre.

Address to the Holy Spirit.

1 ONCE more we come before our God,
 Once more his blessing ask;
O may not duty seem a load;
 Nor worship prove a task!

2 Father, thy quick'ning Spirit send
 From heav'n in JESUS, name,
To make our waiting minds attend,
 And put our souls in frame.

3 To seek thee all our hearts dispose;
 To each thy blessing suit;
And let the seed thy servant sows
 Produce a plenteous fruit.

4 Bid the refreshing north-wind 'wake;
 Say to the south-wind, blow;
Let ev'ry plant thy pow'r partake,
 And all the garden grow.

5 Revive the parch'd with heav'nly show'rs,
 The cold with warmth divine;
And as the benefit is ours,
 Be all the glory thine.

III. Common Metre. (Pf. 5.) A.
For the Lord's Day Morning.

1 LORD, in the morning thou shalt hear
    My voice ascending high;
To thee will I direct my pray'r,
    To thee lift up mine eye.

2 Up to the hills where Christ is gone
    To plead for all his saints,
Presenting at his Father's throne
    Our songs and our complaints.

3 Thou art a God, before whose sight
    The wicked shall not stand;
Sinners shall ne'er be thy delight,
    Nor dwell at thy right-hand.

4 But to thy house will I resort,
    To taste thy mercies there;
I will frequent thine holy court,
    And worship in thy fear.

5 O may thy Spirit guide my feet
    In ways of righteousness!
Make ev'ry path of duty straight,
    And plain before my face.

AT THE OPENING OF

IV. Common Metre.   (Pf. 89.)   *A.*

Reverential Worſhip.

1 WITH rev'rence let the ſaints appear
   And bow before the Lord,
His high commands with rev'rence hear,
   And tremble at his word.

2 How terrible thy glories be!
   How bright thine armies ſhine!
Where is the pow'r that vies with thee?
   Or truth compar'd with thine?

3 The nothern pole and ſouthern reſt
   On thy ſupporting hand.
Darkneſs and day from eaſt to weſt
   Move round at thy command.

4 Thy words the raging winds controul,
   And rule the boiſt'rous deep;
Thou mak'ſt the ſleeping billows roll,
   The rolling billows ſleep.

5 Heav'n, earth and air, and ſea are thine,
   And the dark world of hell:
How did thine arm in vengeance ſhine
When Egypt durſt rebel!

HYMN

HYMN V. Common Metre Steele.   *A.*
Invitation.

1 THE Saviour calls,--- let ev'ry ear
    Attend the heav'nly found;
  Ye doubting fouls, difmifs your fear,
    Hope fmiles reviving round.

2 For ev'ry thirfty, longing heart,
    Here ftreams of bounty flow,
  And life and health, and blifs impart,
    To banifh mortal woe.

3 Here fprings of facred joys arife,
    To eafe your ev'ry pain,
  (Immortal fountain! full fupplies!)
    Nor fhall you thirft in vain.

4 Ye finners, come, 'tis mercy's voice;
    The gracious call obey;
  Mercy invites to heav'nly joys,
    And can you yet delay?

5 Dear Saviour, draw reluctant hearts,
    To thee let finners fly,
  And take the blifs thy love imparts,
    And drink, and never die.

AT THE OPENING OF

HYMN VI. Common Metre. *A.*
Triumphs of Grace.

1 O For a thousand tongues to sing
    My dear Redeemer's praise!
The glories of my God and King,
    The triumphs of his grace.

2 Jesus, the name that charms our fears,
    That bids our sorrow cease;
'Tis music in the sinner's ears,
    'Tis life, and health, and peace.

3 He breaks the pow'r of cancel'd sin,
    He sets the pris'ner free;
His blood can make the foulest clean,
    His blood avail'd for me.

4 He speaks, and list'ning to his voice,
    New life the dead receive;
The mournful, broken heart rejoice,
    The humble poor believe.

5 Hear him, ye deaf; his praise ye dumb,
    Your loosned tongues employ;
Ye blind, behold your Saviour come,
    And leap, ye lame for joy.

HYMN

HYMN VII. Common Metre. *A.*
Book of God's word and Nature.

1 THOU only source of true delight,
    Whom I unseen adore!
Unveil thy beauties to my sight
    That I may love thee more.

2 Thy glory o'er creation shines;
    But in thy sacred word
I read in fairer, brighter lines,
    My bleeding, dying Lord.

3 'Tis here, whene'er my comforts droop,
    And sins and sorrows rise,
Thy love with chearful beams of hope
    My fainting heart supplies.

4 But ah! too soon the pleasing scene
    Is clouded o'er with pain;
My gloomy fears rise dark between,
    And I again complain.

5 Jesus, my Lord, my Life, my Light,
    O come with blissful ray;
Break radiant thro' the shades of night,
    And chase my fears away.

AT THE OPENING OF

HYMN VIII. Common Metre. Dr. Watts. *A.*
God glorified in the Gospel.

1 THE Lord, descending from above,
  Invites his children near;
While pow'r, and truth, and boundless love
  Display their glories here.

2 Here, in thy gospel's wondrous frame,
  Fresh wisdom we pursue;
And thousand angels learn thy name,
  Beyond whate'er they knew.

3 Thy name is writ in fairest lines,
  Thy wonders here we trace;
Wisdom thro' all the myst'ry shines,
  And shines in Jesus' face,

4 The law its best obedience owes
  To our incarnate God!
And thy revenging justice shows
  Its honours in his blood.

5 But still the lustre of thy grace
  Our warmer thoughts employs,
Gilds the whole scene with brightest rays,
  And more exalts our joys.

HYMN

PUBLIC WORSHIP.

HYMN IX. Common Metre. Dr. Watts. *A.*
Praise to God for creation and redemption.

1 LET them neglect thy glory, Lord,
   Who never knew thy grace;
But our loud songs shall still record
   The wonders of thy praise.

2 We raise our shouts, O God, to thee,
   And send them to thy throne;
All glory to th' United Three,
   The undivided One.

3 'Twas he (and we'll adore his name)
   That form'd us by a word;
'Tis he restores our ruin'd frame:
   Salvation to the Lord!

4 Hosanna! let the earth and skies
   Repeat the joyful sound;
Rocks, hills and vales, repeat the voice
   In one eternal round.

HYMN X. Common Metre. Rippon's Coll. *J.*
Heavenly Worship.

1 FREQUENT the day of God returns
   To shed its quick'ning beams;
And yet how slow devotion burns!
   How languid are its flames!

A 5   2 Accept

2 Accept our faint attempts to love,
   Our frailties, Lord forgive;
We would be like thy saints above,
   And praise thee while we live.

3 Increase, O Lord our faith and hope,
   And fit us to ascend,
Where the assembly ne'er breaks up,
   The Sabbath ne'er shall end.

4 Where we shall breathe in heavenly air,
   With heavenly lustre shine;
Before the throne of God appear,
   And feast on love divine.

5 Where we, in high seraphic strains,
   Shall all our powers employ,
Delighted range the etherial plains,
   And take our fill of joy.

HYMN XI. Long Metre, Beddome.   *J.*

Holy Boldness.

1 SPRINKLED with reconciling blood,
   I dare approach thy throne, O God
Thy face no frowning aspect wears,
   Thy hand no vengeful thunder bears!

2 The encircling rainbow, peaceful sign!
   Doth with refulgent brightness shine;

And while my faith beholds it near,
  I bid farewell to ev'ry fear.

3 Let me my grateful homage pay,
    With courage sing; with fervor pray,
  And tho' myself a wretch undone
    Hope for acceptance thro' thy son.

4 Thy son, who on the accursed tree,
    Expir'd to set the vilest free;
  On this I build my only claim,
    And all I ask is in his name.

XII. Long Metre. (Pf. 65.)   J.
Public prayer and praise.

1 THE praise of Zion waits for thee,
    My God; & praise becomes thy house
  There shall thy saints thy glory see,
    And there perform their public vows.

2 O thou, whose mercies bends the skies,
    To save, when humble sinners pray,
  All lands to thee shall lift their eyes,
    And islands of the northern sea.

3 Against my will my sins prevail,
    But grace shall purge away their stain
  The blood of Christ will never fail
    To wash my garments white again.

          A 6   4 Blest

4 Blest is the man whom thou shalt chuse
    And give him kind access to thee;
Give him a place within thy house,
    To taste thy love divinely free.

HYMN XIII. Long Metre. Stennett.   J.
The Sabbath.

1 ANOTHER six days work is done,
    Another sabbath is begun;
Return my soul, enjoy thy rest,
    Improve the day thy God has bless'd

2 Come bless the Lord, whose love assigns.
    So sweet a rest to wearied minds;
Provides an antipast of heaven,
    And gives this day the food of seven.

3 O that our thoughts and thanks might rise
    As greatful incense to the skies.
And draw from heaven that sweet repose
Which none, but he that feels it knows.

4 This heavenly calm, within the breast,
    Is the dear pledge of glorious rest,
Which for the church of God remains
    The end of cares the end of pains.

5 With joy great God, thy works we view
    In various scenes both old and new;

With

With praise, we think on mercies past,
    With hope, we future pleasures taste.

6 In holy duties let the day,
    In holy pleasures pass away;
How sweet, a sabbath thus to spend,
    In hope of one that ne'er shall end!

HYMN XIV. Long Metre. Cowper. *A.*
On Prayer.

1 What various hind'rances we meet
    In coming to a mercy-seat!
Yet who that knows the worth of pray'r
    But wishes to be often there.

2 Prayer makes the darkened cloud withdraw
    Prayer climes the ladder Jacob saw;
Gives exercise to faith and love,
    Brings every blessing from above.

3 Restraining prayer, we cease to fight;
Prayer makes the Christian's armor bright
And satan trembles, when he sees
    The weakest saint upon his knees.

4 While Moses stood with arms spread wide
    Success was found on Israel's side;
But when thro' weariness they fail'd,
    That moment Amalek prevail'd.

5 Have you no words ? ah, think again,
　　Words flow apace when you complain
And fill your fellow-creature's ear
　　With the sad tale of all your care.

HYMN XV.　Long Metre.　Watts.　　A.
Blessing God.

1 BLESS O my soul, the living God
　　Call home thy thoughts that rove
Let all the pow'rs within me join, (abroad
　　In work and worship so divine.

2 Bless, O my soul, the God of grace;
　　His favours claim thy highest praise
Why should the wonders he hath wrought
　　Be lost in silence, and forgot?

3 'Tis he, my soul, that sent his Son
　　To die for crimes which thou hast done
He owns the ransom, and forgives,
　　The hourly follies of our lives.

4 Our youth decay'd his pow'r repairs;
　　His mercy crowns our growing years
He satisfies our mouths with good,
　　And fills our hopes with heav'nly food.

5 Let the whole earth his pow'r confess,
　　Let the whole earth adore his grace,
　　　　　　　　　　　　　　　　The

The *Gentile* with the *Jew* shall join
  In work and worship so divine.

HYMN XVI. Long Metre. Rippon. Coll. A.
Loving kindness of God.

1 AWAKE my soul, in joyful lays
   And sing thy great Redeemer's praise
  He justly claims a song from me,
   His loving kindness O how free!

2 He saw me ruin'd in the fall
   Yet loved notwithstanding all;
  He sav'd me from my lost estate
   His loving kindness O how great!

3 Often I feel my sinful heart,
   Prone from my Jesus to depart;
  But tho' I have him oft' forgot,
   His loving kindness changes not,

4 Soon shall I pass the gloomy vale,
   Soon all my mortal powers must fail
  Oh! may my last expiring breath,
   His loving kindness sing in death.

5 Then let me mount and soar away,
   To the bright worlds of endless day,
  And sing with rapture and surprise,
   His loving kindness in the skies.

HYMN XVII. Long Metre. Dr. Watts.   *A.*
Invitation of Christ.

1 "COME hither, all ye weary souls
   "Ye heavy laden sinners come;
   "I'll give you rest from all your toils,
   "And raise you to my heav'nly home.

2 "They shall find rest that learn of me;
   "I'm of a meek and lowly mind;
   "But passion rages like the sea,
   "And pride is restless as the wind.

3 "Bless'd is the man whose shoulders take
   "My yoke, and bear it with delight;
   "My yoke is easy to his neck,
   "My grace shall make the burden light."

4 JESUS, we come at thy command;
   With faith and hope, and humble zeal
   Resign our spirits to thy hand,
   To mould and guide us by thy will.

HYMN XVIII. Long Metre. Beddome.   *A.*
Craving the Spirit.

1 Come gracious Spirit, heavenly dove,
   With light and comfort from above
   Be thou our guardian, thou our guide
   O'er every thought and step preside

2 Conduct

2 Conduct us safe, conduct us far,
   From every sin and hurtful snare;
Lead to thy word that rules must give
   And teach us lessons how to live.

3 The light of truth to us display,
   And make us know and chuse thy way
Plant holy fear in every heart
That we from God, may ne'er depart.

4 Lead us to holiness, the road,
   That we must take to dwell with God
Lead us to Christ the living way,
   Nor let us from his pastures stray.

5 Lead us to God, our final rest,
   In his enjoyment to be bless'd
Lead us to Heaven, the seat of bliss,
   Where pleasure in perfection is.

HYMN XIX. Long Metre.   *A.*

Exhorting to Worship.

1 BEFORE JEHOVAH's awful throne,
   Ye nations, bow with sacred joy;
Know that the Lord is God alone,
   He can create and he destroy.

2 His sov'reign pow'r without our aid,
   Made us of clay, and form'd us men

And when like wand'ring sheep we stray'd
He brought us to his fold again.

3 We'll croud thy gates with thankful songs
High as the heav'ns our voices raise;
And earth with her ten thousand tongues
Shall fill thy courts with sounding praise.

4 Wide as the world is thy command;
Vast as eternity thy love;
Firm as a rock thy truth must stand,
When rolling years shall cease to move.

XX. Long Metre. (Psalm 100.) *J.*

Praise to our Creator.

1 YE nations round the earth, rejoice
Before the Lord, your sov'reign King
Serve him with chearful heart and voice,
With all your tongues his glory sing.

2 The Lord is God; 'tis he alone
Doth life, and breath, and being give,
We are his work, and not our own;
The sheep that on his pastures live.

3 Enter his gates with songs of joy,
With praises to his courts repair,
And make it your divine employ,
To pay your thanks and honours there.

4 The

4 The Lord is good, the Lord is kind;
    Great is his grace, his mercy sure:
And the whole race of man shall find
    His truth from age to age endure.

HYMN XXI. Short Metre. Dr. Watts. J.
    Delight in Public Worship.

1 WELCOME sweet day of rest
        That saw the Lord arise;
    Welcome to this reviving breast,
        And these rejoicing eyes!

2 The King himself comes near,
        And feasts his saints to-day;
    Here we may sit, and see him here,
        And love, and praise, and pray.

3 One day amidst the place
        Where my dear God hath been,
    Is sweeter than ten thousand days
        Of pleasurable sin.

4 My willing soul would stay
        In such a frame as this,
    And sit and sing herself away
        To everlasting bliss.

HYMN

AT THE OPENING OF

HYMN XXII. Short Metre. Hart.   *A.*
Invoking the Spirit.

1 COME, Holy Spirit, come,
　　Let thy bright beams arise;
　Dispel the darkness from our minds,
　　And open all our eyes.

2 Chear our desponding hearts,
　　Thou heav'nly Paraclete,
　Give us to lie, with humble hope,
　　At our Redeemer's feet.

3 Revive our drooping faith,
　　Our doubts and fears remove;
　And kindle in our breasts the flames
　　Of never dying love.

4 Convince us of our sin,
　　Then lead to Jesus' blood;
　And to our wond'ring view reveal
　　The secret love of God.

5 Shew us that loving Man,
　　That rules the courts of bliss,
　The Lord of hosts the mighty God,
　　The eternal Prince of Peace:

HYNM

HYMN XXIII. Short Metre. Dr. Watts. A.
Heavenly joy on earth.

1 [COME, we that love the Lord,
 And let our joys be known;
Join in a song with sweet accord,
 And thus surround the throne.

2 The sorrows of the mind
 Be banish'd from this place:
Religion never was design'd
 To make our pleasures less.]

3 Let those refuse to sing,
 That never knew our God,
But fav'rites of the heav'nly King
 May speak their joys abroad.

4 This heav'nly King is ours
 Our Father and our love;
He shall send down his heav'nly pow'rs
 To carry us above.

5 There shall we see his face,
 And never, never sin;
There from the rivers of his grace,
 Drink endless pleasures in.

XXIV.

AT THE OPENING OF

XXIV. Short Metre. (Pſ. 95.) A.
Exhortation to Praiſe.

1 COME, ſound his praiſe abroad,
    And hymns of glory ſing;
Jehovah is the ſov'reign God,
    The univerſal King.

2 He form'd the deeps unknown;
    He gave the ſeas their bound;
The wat'ry worlds are all his own:
    And all the ſolid ground.

3 Come, worſhip at his throne,
    Come, bow before the Lord:
We are his works, and not our own:
    He form'd us by his word.

4 But if your ears refuſe
    The language of his grace,
And hearts grown hard, like ſtubborn Jews
    That unbelieving race;

5 The Lord in vengeance dreſt
    Will lift his hand and ſwear,
You that deſpiſe my promis'd reſt,
    Shall have no portion there

HYMN

PUBLIC WORSHIP. 23

HYMN XXV. Short Metre. A.
Heavenly Praise.

1 SALVATION to our God,
Who sitteth on the throne;
Thanks giving to the Holy Ghost,
And to the Lamb, the Son.

2 All glory, praise, and pow'r.
To God be ever given,
By every Angel round the throne
And all the hosts of heaven.

3 Great are thy wondrous works!
Most just and true thy ways;
Lord God Almighty King of saints,
High in eternal praise.

4 Who shall not fear thy might?
By every pow'r ador'd;
All nations shall before thee kneel,
And gladly call thee Lord.

HYMN XXVI. Common Metre. Lyric Poems. J.
A Song to Creating Wisdom.

1 ETERNAL WISDOM thee we praise
Thee the creation sings
With thy lov'd name, rocks, hills & seas
And heav'ns high palace rings.

2 Thy hand how wide it spreads the sky!
  How glorious to behold!
Ting'd with a blue and heavenly dye,
  And starr'd with sparkling gold.

3 Thy glorious blaze all nature round,
  And strike the gazing sight,
'Thro' skies, and seas, and solid ground
  With terror and delight.

4 Infinite strength and equal skill,
  Shine thro' the worlds abroad,
Our souls with vast amazement fill,
  And speak the builder GOD.

5 But the sweet beauties of thy grace
  Our softer passions move;
Pity divine in *JESUS*' face
  We see, adore, and love.

HYMN XXVII.   Common Metre. Steel. *J.*
Creation and Providence.

1 LORD when our Raptur'd thought
    Creation's beauties o'er (surveys
  All nature joins to teach thy praise,
    And bid our souls adore.

2 Where'er we turn our gazing eyes,
    Thy radiant footsteps shine;

Ten thousand pleasing wonders rise,
And speak their source divine.

3 The living tribes of countless forms,
In earth and sea and air.
The meanest flies the smallest worms,
Almighty power declare.

4 Thy wisdom, pow'r and goodness Lord
In all thy works appear;
And O! let man thy praise record,
Man, thy distinguish'd care.

5 Thy providence his constant guard,
When threatning woes impend,
Or will the impending dangers ward
Or timely succours lend.

6 On us that providence has shone,
With gentle smiling rays
O, may our lips and lives make known
Thy goodness and thy praise.

HYMN XXVIII. Common Metre. Steel. *J.*
The Excellency of the Scripture.

1 FATHER of mercies, in thy word
What endless glory shines?
For ever be thy name ador'd,
For these celestial lines.

2 Here the fair tree of knowledge grows,
    And yields a free repast;
Sublimer sweets than nature knows,
    Invite the longing taste.

3 Here springs of consolation rise,
    To chear the fainting mind;
And thirsty souls receive supplies,
    And sweet refreshment find.

4 Here the Redeemer's welcome voice
    Spreads heav'nly peace around;
And life, and everlasting joys
    Attend the blissful sound.

5 O may these heav'nly pages be
    My ever dear delight,
And still new beauties may I see,
    And still increasing light.

6 Divine instructor, gracious Lord!
    Be thou for ever near;
Teach me to love thy sacred word,
    And view my Saviour there.

HYMN XXIX. Common Metre. *J.*
For a clean Heart.

1 O For an heart to love my God!
    An heart from sin set free;

An heart that always feels the blood
    So freely shed for me!

2 An heart resign'd submissive, meek,
    My dear Redeemer's throne;
Where only CHRIST is heard to speak,
    Where JESUS reigns alone.

3 An humble, lowly, contrite heart,
    Believing, true, and clean;
Which neither life nor death can part
    From him that dwells within.

4 An heart in every thought renew'd
    And fill'd with love divine:
Perfect and right and pure and good,
    A copy, LORD, of thine.

5 Thy tender heart is still the same,
    And melts at human woe;
Send down thy grace, O blessed Lamb,
    That I thy love may know.

6 Thy holy nature, LORD! impart;
    Come quickly from above;
Write thy new name upon my heart,
    Thy new best name of love.

HYMN

BEFORE SERMON.

HYMN. XXX. Common Metre. Steel. J.
The Joys of Heaven.

1 COME, Lord, and warm each
    languid heart,
Inspire each lifeless tongue;
    And let the joys of heaven impart
Their influ'nce to our song.

2 Then to the shining seats of bliss
    The wings of faith shall soar,
And all the charms of paradise
    Our raptur'd thoughts explore,

3 Pleasures unsully'd flourish there,
    Beyond the reach of time;
Not blooming Eden smil'd so fair
    In all her flow'ry prime.

4 Sorrow and pain, and ev'ry care
    And discord there shall cease;
And perfect joy and love sincere
    Adorn the realms of peace.

5 The soul, from sin for ever free,
    shall mourn its pow'r no more;
But cloth'd in spotless purity,
    Redeeming love adore.

6 There shall the followers of the Lamb,
     Join in immortal songs;
  And endless honours to his name
     Employ their tuneful tongues.

7 Lord, tune our hearts to praise & love
     Our feeble notes inspire;
  Till in thy blissful courts above
     We join th' angelic choir.

HYMN XXXI. Common Metre. Dr. Watts,
Breathing after the holy Spirit.

1 COME, holy Spirit, heav'nly Dove
     With all thy quick'ning pow'rs;
  Kindle a flame of sacred love
     In these cold hearts of ours.

2 Look how we grovel here below,
     Fond of these trifling toys;
  Our souls can neither fly, nor go
     To reach eternal joys.

3 In vain we tune our formal songs,
     In vain we strive to rise;
  Hosannas languish on our tongues,
     And our devotion dies.

4 Dear Lord, and shall we ever lie
     At this poor dying rate?
                              Our

Our love so faint, so cold to thee,
And thine to us so great?

5 Come, holy Spirit, heav'nly Dove,
With all thy quick'ning pow'rs;
Come shed abroad a Saviours's love,
And that shall kindle ours.

HYMN XXXII. Common Metre. Dr. Gibbons. J.
The gospel worthy of all acceptance.

1 JESUS the eternal Son of God,
Whom seraphim obey,
The bosom of the Father leaves,
And enters human clay.

2 Into our sinful world he comes
The Messenger of grace.
And on the bloody tree expires
A victim in our place.

3 Transgressors of the deepest stain
In him salvation find;
His blood removes the foulest guilt,
His spirit heals the mind.

4 Our Jesus saves from sin and hell,
His words are true and sure,
And on this rock our faith may rest
Immoveably secure.

5 O let

5 O let these Tidings be receiv'd,
  With universal joy,
 And let the high angel praise,
  Our tuneful pow'rs employ,

6 "Glory to God, who gave his son"
  To bear our shame and pain,
 Hence peace on earth and grace to men
  In endless blessings reign.

XXXIII. Common Metre. (Pf. 145.)   J.
The goodness of God.

1 SWEET is the mem'ry of thy grace,
  My GOD, my heav'nly King!
 Let age to age thy righteousness
  In founds of glory sing.

2 GOD reigns on high, but not confines
  His goodness to the skies;
 Thro' the whole earth his goodness shines
  And ev'ry want supplies.

3 With longing eyes thy creatures wait
  On thee for daily food;
 Thy lib'ral hand provides them meat,
  And fills their mouths with good.

4 How kind are thy compassions, LORD,
  How slow thine anger moves!

But

32 BEFORE SERMON.

But soon he sends his pard'ning word,
  To chear the soul he loves.

5 Creatures, with all their endless race,
  Thy pow'r and praise proclaim:
May we, who taste thy richer grace,
  Delight to bless thy name.

HYMN XXXIV. Common Metre. Lyric Poems. *A Looking upward.*

1 EARTH has detain'd me prisoner
    And I'm grown weary now (long
  My heart, my hand, my ear my tongue
    There's nothing here for you.

2 Lord in my thoughts I stretch me down
    And upwards glance mine eyes.
  Upward (my Father) to thy throne,
    And to my native skies.

3 There the dear Man my Saviour sits,
    The GOD, how bright he shines!
  And scatters infinite delights
    On all the happy minds.

4 Seraphs with elevated strains
    Circle the throne around.
  And move and charm the starry plains
    With an immortal sound.

                                5 JESUS

5 Jesus the Lord their harps employs,
    Jesus my love they sing.
Jesus the name of both our joys
    Sounds sweet from every string.

XXXV. Common Metre. (Pf. 116.)   *A*
Thankfulness for mercies.

1 WHAT shall I render to my God
    For all his kindness shown?
My feet shall visit thine abode,
    My songs address thy throne.

2 Among the saints that fill thine house,
    My off'rings shall be paid;
There shall my zeal perform the vows
    My soul in anguish made.

3 How much is mercy thy delight,
    Thou ever blessed God!
How dear thy servants in thy sight!
    How precious is their blood?

4 How happy all thy servants are!
    How great thy grace to me?
My life, which thou hast made thy care
    Lord, I devote to thee.

5 Now I am thine, for ever thine
    Nor shall my purpose move;

Thy hand hath loos'd my bonds of pain,
And bound me with thy love.

XXXVI. Common Metre. (Pſ. 69.)   *A.*
Obedience and Death of Chriſt.

1 FATHER, I ſing thy wond'rous grace
    I bleſs my Saviour's name.
He bought ſalvation for the poor,
    And bore the ſinners ſhame.

2 His deep diſtreſs has rais'd us high;
    His duty and his zeal.
Fulfill'd the law which mortals broke,
    And finiſh'd all thy will.

3 His dying groans, his living ſongs,
    Shall better pleaſe my God,
Than harp or trumpet's ſolemn ſound,
    Than goats or bullocks blood.

4 This ſhall his humble foll'wers ſee,
    And ſet their hearts at reſt;
They by his death draw near to thee.
    And live for ever bleſt.

5 Let heav'n, and all that dwell on high,
    To God their voices raiſe,
While lands and ſeas aſſiſt the ſky,
    And join'd t' advance thy praiſe.

XXXVII. Common Metre. (Pſ. 84.) *A.*
Gods preſence in his Houſe.

1 MY ſoul how lovely is the place
    To which thy God reſorts?
'Tis heav'n to ſee his ſmiling face,
    Though in his earthly courts.

2 There the great Monarch of the ſkies
    His ſaving pow'r diſplays,
And light breaks in upon our eyes,
    With kind and quick'ning rays.

3 With his rich gifts the heav'nly dove
    Deſcends and fills the place,
While Chriſt reveals his wond'rous love
    And ſheds abroad his grace.

4 There mighty God, thy works declare
    The ſecrets of thy will;
And ſtill we ſeek thy mercy there,
    And ſing thy praiſes ſtill.

HYMN XXXVIII. Common Metre. Beddome. *A.*
Fear Not.

1 YE trembling ſouls diſmiſs your fears
    Be mercy all your theme;
Mercy which like a river flows,
    In one continued ſtream.

2 Fear not the powers of earth and hell,
    God will these powers restrain;
His mighty arm their rage repel,
    And make their efforts vain,

3 Fear not the want of outward good,
    He will for his provide;
Grant them supplies of daily food,
    And give them heaven beside.

4 Fear not that he will e'er forsake,
    Or leave his work undone;
He's faithful to his promises,
    And faithful to his son.

5 You in his wisdom, power and grace,
    May confidently trust;
His wisdom guides, his power protects,
    His grace rewards the just.

HYMN XXXIX. Common Metre. Dr. Stennett. *J.*

The glorious Gospel 1 Tim. I. II.

1 WHAT Wisdom Majesty and grace
    Thro' all the Gospel shine!
'Tis GOD that speaks, and we confess
    The Doctrine most divine.

2 Down from his starry Throne on high,
    Th' Almighty Saviour comes;

Lays his bright robes of glory by,
   And feeble flesh assumes.

3 The mighty debt that sinners owe,
   Upon the cross he pays:
Then thro' the clouds ascends to God,
   'Midst shouts of lofty praise.

4 There he our great high priest appears,
   Before his father's throne:
Mingles his merits with our tears,
   And pours salvation down.

5 Great GOD, with rev'rence we adore
   Thy Justice and thy grace;
And on thy faithfulness and power
   Our firm dependence place.

XL.   Common Metre.   (Ps. viii.)   J.
Condescension of God.

1 O Lord, our Lord, how wond'rous
      Is thine exalted name,   (great,
The glories of thy heav'nly state,
   Let men and babes proclaim.

2 When I behold thy works on high,
   The moon that rules the night,
And stars that well adorn the sky,
   Those moving worlds of light:

B   3 Lord,

3 Lord, what is man, or all his race,
　Who dwells so far below,
That thou should'st visit him with grace,
　And love his nature so?

4 That thine eternal Son should bear,
　To take a mortal form?
Made lower than his angels are,
　To save a dying worm?

5 Jesus, our Lord, how wond'rous great
　Is thine exalted name!
The glories of thy heav'nly state
　Let the whole earth proclaim.

XLI. Long Metre. (Ps. lxiii.)　　J.
Longing after God.

1 GREAT God, indulge my humble claim
　Be thou my joy, my hope my rest
The glories that compose thy name,
　Stand all engag'd to make me blest.

2 Thou great, good, thou just and wise,
　Be thou my father and my God;
And make me thine by sacred ties,
　Thy Son thy servant bought with blood

3 With heart and eyes and lifted hands,
　For thee I long, to thee I look;

As travellers in thirsty lands,
   Pant for the cooling water brook.

4 O may thy love inspire my tongue,
   Salvation shall be all my song;
And all my powers shall join to bless,
The Lord my strength and Righteousness.

XLII. Long Metre. (Pſ. cxxxvi.)   J.
Creation and Redemption.

1 GIVE to our God immortal praise:
   Mercy and truth are all his ways;
Wonders of grace to God belong,
Repeat his mercies in your song.

2 Give to the Lord of lords renown,
The King of kings with glory crown
His mercies ever shall endure,
When lords & kings are known no more.

3 He built the earth he spread the sky,
And fix'd the starry lights on high:
Wonders of grace to God belong,
Repeat his mercies in your song.

4 He fills the sun with morning light;
He bids the moon direct the night;
His mercies ever shall endure,
When suns and moons shall be no more.

5 He sent his Son with power to save,
From guilt and darkness and the grave,
Wonders of grace to God belong,
Repeat his mercies in your song.

6 Through this vain world he guides our
And leads us to his heav'nly seat (feet
His mercies ever shall endure,
When this vain world shall be no more

XLIII. Long Metre. Lyric Poems.   J.
God exalted above all praise.

1 ETERNAL power, whose high abode
Becomes the grandeur of a God,
Infinite length, beyond the bounds
Where stars revolve their little rounds.

2 The lowest step above thy seat,
Rises too high for Gabriel's feet.
In vain the tall arch-angel tries;
To reach the hight with wond'ring eyes.

3 Lord, what shall earth and ashes do?
We would adore our maker too;
From sin and dust to thee we cry,
The great, the holy, and the high.

4 Earth from afar, has heard thy fame,
And worms have learnt to lisp thy name
But

But O, the glories of thy mind.
Leave all our soaring thoughts behind.

5 God is in heaven, but men below;
Be short our tunes our words be few,
A sacred rev'rence checks our songs,
And praise sits silent on our tongues.

XLIV. Long Metre. Rippon's Coll.   J.
Spirituality of God.

1 THOU art O God! a spirit pure,
    Invisible to mortal eyes,
Th' immortal, and the eternal King,
    The great, the good, the only wise.

2 Whilst nature changes, and her works
    Corrupt, decay, dissolve and die,
Thy essence pure no change shall see,
    Secure of immortality.

3 Thou great Invisible! what hand
    Can draw thy image spotless fair?
To what in Heaven, to what on earth,
    Can men th' immortal king compare.

4 Let stupid heathens frame their gods,
    Of gold and silver, wood and stone
Ours is the God that made the Heavens,
    Jehovah he, and God alone.

5 My soul, thy purest homage pay,
In truth and Spirit him adore,
More shall this please than sacrifice,
Than outward forms, delight him more.

XLV. Long Metre. Dr. Doddridge. J.
Immutability of God.

1 GREAT Former of this various frame
Our souls adore thine awful name;
And bow and tremble, while they praise
The ancient of eternal days.

2 Thou, Lord, with unsurpris'd survey,
Saw'st nature rising yesterday;
And, as tomorrow, shall thine eye,
See earth and stars in ruin lie.

3 Beyond an angel's vision bright,
Thou dwell'st in self-existent light,
Which shines with undiminish'd ray,
While suns and worlds in smoke decay.

4 Our days a transient period run,
And change with ev'ry circling sun,
And in the firmest state we boast,
A moth can crush us into dust.

5 But let the creatures fall around;
Let death consign us to the ground,

Let

BEFORE SERMON.

Let the laſt general flame ariſe,
And melt the Arches of the ſkies:

6 Calm as the ſummer's ocean, we,
Can all the wreck of nature ſee,
While grace ſecures us an abode,
Unſhaken as the throne of God.

XLVI. Long Metre. Dr. Doddridge. J.
The goſpel Jubilee. (Pſ. lxxxv. 15.)

1 LOUD let the tuneful trumpet ſound
And ſpread the joyful tidings round
Let every ſoul with tranſport hear,
And hail the Lord's accepted year.

2 Ye Debtors whom he gives to know,
That you ten thouſand talents owe,
When humble at his feet you fall,
Your gracious GOD forgives them all

3 Slaves, that have borne the heavy Chain
Of ſin and Hell's tyrannic reign,
To liberty aſſert your claim,
And urge the great Redeemer's name.

4 The rich inheritance of Heaven,
Your joy, and boaſt, is freely given,
Fair Salem your arrival waits,
With golden ſtreets and pearly gates.

B 4 5 Her

5 Her bless'd inhabitants no more,
   Bondage and poverty deplore;
No Debt, but love immensely great,
   Their Joy still rises with their Debt.

6 O happy Souls that know the sound!
   Celestial Light their steps surround,
And shew that Jubilee begun,
   Which thro' eternal Years shall run.

HYMN XLVII. Long Metre.   J.
The Lord is God.

1 DOES it not grief and wonder move
   To think of Israel's' dreadful fall,
Who needed miracles to prove
   Whether the Lord were God or Baal.

2 Methinks I see Elijah stand,
   His features glow with love and zeal
In faith and prayer he lifts his hand,
   And makes to heav'n his great appeal.

"O GOD! if I thy servant am,
   If 'tis thy message fills my heart;
Now glorify thy holy name:
   And shew this people who thou art.

4 He spoke, and lo! a sudden flame,
   Consum'd the wood, the dust, the stone

                          The

The people struck, at once proclaim,
  "The Lord is God, the Lord alone."

5 Like him we mourn an awful day,
    When more for Baal than God appear
  Like him, believers, let us pray,
    And may the God of Israel hear.

6 Lord! If thy servant speaks thy truth,
    If he indeed is sent by thee;
  Confirm the word to all our youth,
    And let them thy salvation see.

7 Now may thy Spirit's holy fire,
    Pierce ev'ry heart that hears thy word
  Consume each hurtful vain desire,
    And make them know thou art the Lord.

XLVIII. Long Metre. (Ps. xix.)   J.
The Books of Nature and of the Scripture.

1 THE heav'ns declare thy glory Lord,
    In every star thy wisdom shines:
  But when our eyes behold thy word,
    We read thy name in fairer lines.

2 The rolling sun, the changing light,
    And nights and days thy power confess,
  But the blest volume thou hast writ,
    Reveals thy justice and thy grace.

3 Sun, moon, and stars; convey thy praise
  Round the whole earth, and never stand
  So when thy truth begun its race,
  It touch'd and glanc'd on ev'ry land.

4 Nor shall thy spreading gospel rest,
  'Till through the world thy truth has run,
  'Till Christ has all the nations blest,
  That see the light, or feel the sun.

5 Great Sun of Righteousness, arise,
  Bless the dark world with heav'nly light,
  Thy gospel makes the simple wise:
  Thy laws are pure, thy judgments right.

6 Thy noblest wonders here we view,
  In souls renew'd and sins forgiv'n;
  Lord cleanse my sins, my soul renew,
  And make thy word my guide to heav'n.

XLIX. Long Metre. (Ps. xxxvi.)   J.
Providence and Grace.

1 HIGH in the heav'ns, eternal God,
     Thy goodness in full glory shines
  Thy truth shall break through ev'ry cloud
     That veils and darkens thy designs.

2 For ever firm thy justice stands,
     As mountains their foundations keep,
                    Wise

BEFORE SERMON.   47

    Wife are the wonders of thy hands,
        Thy judgments are a mighty deep.

3 Thy providence is kind and large,
    Both man and beaft thy bounty fhare
  The whole creation is thy charge,
    But faints are thy peculiar care.

4 My God! how excellent thy grace,
    Whence all my hope and comfort
  The fons of Adam in diftrefs, (fprings,
    Fly to the fhadow of thy wings.

5 From the provifions of thy houfe
    We fhall be fed with fweet repaft;
  There mercy like a river flows,
    And brings Salvation to our tafte.

6 Life, like a fountain rich and free,
    Springs from the prefence of my Lord,
  And in thy light our fouls fhall fee,
    The glories promis'd in thy word.

L.   Long Metre. (Pf. xlv.)   A.
Chrift and his Church.

1 THE king of faints, how fair his face
    Adorn'd with majefty and grace,
  He comes with bleffings from above,
    And wins the nations to his love.

2 At his right hand our eyes behold,
The queen array'd in pureſt gold;
The world admires her heav'nly dreſs,
Her robe of joy and Righteouſneſs.

3 He forms her beauties like his own ;
He calls and ſeats her near his throne
Fair ſtranger, let thine heart forget
The idols of thy native ſtate.

4 So ſhall the king the more rejoice,
In thee, the fav'rite of his choice;
Let Him be lov'd and yet ador'd,
For He's thy maker and thy Lord.

5 Let endleſs honours crown his head ;
Let ev'ry age his praiſes ſpread ;
While we with chearful ſongs approve,
The condeſcenſions of his love.

LI.   Long Metre.   (Pſ. lxviii.)   A.
Aſcenſion of Chriſt.

1 Lord, when thou didſt aſcend on high
Ten thouſand angels fill'd the ſky,
Thoſe heav'nly guards around thee wait
Like chariots that attend thy ſtate.

2 Not Sinai's mountain could appear,
More glorious, when the Lord was there;

While

While he pronounc'd his dreadful law,
And struck the chosen tribes with awe.

3 How bright the triumph none can tell,
When the rebellious pow'rs of hell,
That thousand souls had captives made
Were all in chains like captives led.

4 Rais'd by his father to the throne,
He sent the promis'd Spirit down,
With gifts and grace for rebel men,
That God might dwell on earth again.

HYMN LII. Long Metre. Dr. Watts. *A Holy walk.*

1 SO let our lips and lives express,
  The holy gospel we profess:
So let our works and virtues shine,
  To prove the doctrine all divine.

2 Thus shall we best proclaim abroad,
  The honours of our Saviour God:
When the salvation reigns within,
  And grace subdues the power of sin.

3 Our flesh and sense must be deny'd,
  Passion and envy, lust and pride;
Whilst justice, temp'rance truth, & love,
  Our inward piety approve.

B 7   4 Religion

4 Religion bears our spirits up,
While we expect that blessed hope,
The bright appearance of the LORD,
And faith stands leaning on his word.

HYMN LIII. Long Metre. Dr. Watts. *A.*
Devout retirement.

1 FAR from my thoughts vain world be gone,
Let my religious hours alone;
Fain would my eyes my Saviour see,
I wait a visit, Lord, from thee.

2 My heart grows warm with holy fire,
And kindles with a pure desire:
Come my dear Jesus, from above,
And feed my soul with heav'nly love.

3 O haste, but with a smiling face,
And spread the table of thy grace;
Bring down a taste of truth divine,
And cheer my heart with sacred wine.

4 Bless'd Jesus, what delicious fare!
How sweet thy entertainments are!
Never did angels taste above,
Redeeming grace and dying love.

5 Hail

5 Hail great Immanuel, all divine!
In thee thy Father's glories shine;
Thou brightest, sweetest, fairest one,
That eyes have seen, or angels known.

HYMN LIV. Long Metre. Dr. Watts. A.
Encouragement to wait on God.

1 THUS saith the wisdom of the Lord,
Bless'd is the man that hears my word;
Keeps daily watch before my gates,
And at my feet for mercy waits.

2 The soul that seeks me shall obtain
Immortal wealth, and heav'nly gain,
Immortal life is his reward,
Life, and the favour of the Lord.

3 But the vile wretch that flies from me,
Doth his own soul an injury;
Fools that against my grace rebel,
Seek death, and love the road to hell.

HYMN LV. Long Metre. Dr. S. Stennett. J.
Gods reasoning with men. Is. i. 18.

1 COME sinners, saith the mighty God
Heinous as all your Crimes have been

BEFORE SERMON.

Lo! I descend from mine abode
To reason with the sons of men.

2 No clouds of darkness veil my face,
   No vengeful lightnings flash around
I come with terms of life and peace;
Where sin hath reign'd let grace abound.

3 Yes, LORD, we will obey thy call,
   And to thy gracious Sceptre bow;
O make our crimson sins like wool,
   Our scarlet sins as white as snow.

4 So shall our thankful lips repeat
   Thy praises with a tuneful voice,
While, humbly prostrate at thy feet,
   We wonder, tremble, and rejoice.

HYMN LVI. Long Metre. Doddridge.   A.
A Joyful Course.

1 Assist us, LORD, thy name to praise
   For the rich gospel of thy grace;
And, that our hearts may love it more,
Teach them to feel its vital power.

2 With joy may we our course pursue,
And keep the crown of life in view;
That crown, which in one hour repays
The labour of ten thousand days.

3 Should

3 Should bonds or death obstruct our way
   Unmov'd their terrors we'll survey;
   And the last hour improve for thee,
   The last of life, or liberty.

4 Welcome those bonds, which may unite
   Our souls to their supreme delight!
   Welcome that death whose painful strife
   Bears us to CHRIST our better life!

LVII. Common Metre. (Pf. cxix.)   A.
Breathing after Holiness.

1 O that the Lord would guide my ways
      To keep his statutes still!
   O that my GOD would grant me grace
      To know and do his will!

2 O send thy Spirit down to write
      Thy law upon my heart!
   Nor let my tongue indulge deceit,
      Nor act the liar's part.

3 From vanity turn off my eyes;
      Let no corrupt design,
   Nor covetous desires arise
      Within this soul of mine.

BEFORE SERMON.

4 Order my footsteps by thy word,
    And make my heart sincere;
Let sin have no dominion, Lord,
    But keep my conscience clear.

5 Make me to walk in thy commands,
    'Tis a delightful road;
Nor let my head, or heart, or hands
    Offend against my God.

HYMN LVIII. ~~Short~~ Metre. *A.*

Christ precious.

1 I Love thy charming name,
    'Tis music to my ear;
Fain would I sound it out so loud
    That earth and heav'n might hear

2 Yes thou art precious to my soul,
    My transport and my trust,
Jewels to thee are gaudy toys,
    And gold is sordid dust.

3 All my capacious pow'rs can wish
    In thee most richly meet;
Nor to my eyes is light so dear,
    Nor friedship half so sweet.

4 O may thy grace still cheer my heart,
  And shed its fragrance there!
The noblest balm of all its wounds,
  The cordial of its care.

5 I'll speak the honours of thy name
  With my last lab'ring breath;
When speechless clasp thee in mine arms
  My joy in life and death!

HYMN LIX. Short Metre. *A.*
A preached Word.

1 WITH heart and lips unfeign'd,
  We praise thee for thy word;
We bless thee for the joyful news
  Of our redeeming LORD.

2 O let thy present voice,
  Accomplish thy design,
Distil on all our thirsty souls,
  And consecrate us thine.

3 Water thy sacred seed,
  And give it great increase;
Let neither fowls nor rocks nor thorns,
  Hinder the fruits of peace.

4 Then tho' we weeping sow,
  And tears our hearts employ;

We

We know we shall return again,
　　　　　And bring our sheaves with joy.
5 Our lives now hid with Christ,
　　　　　With him shall soon appear;
　　　And we array'd in all his light,
　　　　　Shall meet him in the air.

　　　　LX. Common Metre. (Pf. lxxxix.)　　J.
　　　　　　A blessed Gospel.

1 **B**lest are the souls that hear and know
　　　　　The gospel's joyful sound;
　　　Peace shall attend the path they go,
　　　　　And light their steps surround.

2 Their joy shall bear their spirits up
　　　　　Thro' their Redeemer's name;
　　　His righteousness exalts their hope,
　　　　　Nor satan dares condemn.

3 The Lord our glory and defence
　　　　　Strength and salvation gives:
　　　Israel, thy King for ever reigns,
　　　　　Thy God for ever lives.

　　　　　　　　　　　　　　　　HYMN

AFTER SERMON.

HYMN LXI. Common Metre. *J.*

Grace.

1 Rich grace, free grace most sweetly calls
    Directly come who will;
Just as you are, for CHRIST receives
    Poor helpless sinners still.

2 'Tis grace each day that feeds our souls;
    grace keeps us inly poor;
And, O! that nothing else but grace
    May rule for evermore.

LXII. Common Metre. (Pf. cxxx.) *J.*

Pardoning Grace.

1 OUT of the deeps of long distress,
    The borders of despair,
I sent my cries to seek thy grace,
    My groans to move thine ear.

2 Great God, should thy severer eye,
    And thine impartial hand,
Mark and revenge iniquity,
    No mortal flesh could stand.

3 But there are pardons with my God
    For crimes of high degree;
Thy Son has bought them with his blood
    To draw us near to thee.

4 Then

4 Then in the Lord let Israel trust,
    Let Israel seek his face;
The Lord is good as well as just,
    And plenteous is his grace.

5 There's full redemption at his throne
    For sinners long enslav'd;
The great Redeemer is his Son,
    And Israel shall be sav'd.

HYMN LXIII. Common Metre. Toplady. *J.*
Christ's Intercession.

1 AWAKE, sweet gratitude and sing,
    Th' ascended Saviour's love;
Sing how he lives to carry on,
    His people's cause above.

2 For all that come to God by him,
    Salvation he demands;
Points to their names upon his breast,
    And spreads his wounded hands.

3 His sweet atoning sacrifice,
    Gives sanction to his claim:
" Father, I will that all my saints,
" Be with me where I am:

4 " By their salvation, recompense,
" The sorrows I endur'd;
                              " Just

AFTER SERMON.

"Juſt to the merits of thy Son,
"And faithful to thy word."

5 Eternal life, at his requeſt,
    To every ſaint is given:
Safety on Earth, and, after death,
    The plenitude of Heaven.

HYMN LXIV. Common Metre. Dr. Watts. J.
The Reſurrection of Chriſt.

1 HOSANNA to the Prince of light
    That cloth'd himſelf in clay;
Enter'd the iron gates of death,
    And tore the bars away.

2 Death is no more the king of dread,
    Since our Immanuel roſe;
He took the tyrant's ſting away,
    And ſpoil'd our helliſh foes.

3 See how the Conqu'ror mounts aloft,
    And to his Father flies,
With ſcars of honour in his fleſh,
    And triumph in his eyes.

4 Raiſe your devotion, mortal tongues,
    To reach his bleſs'd abode;
Sweet be the accents of our ſongs,
    To our incarnate God.

5 Bright

5 Bright angels, strike your loudest string
  Your sweetest voices raise;
Let heav'n and all created things,
  Sound our Immanuel's praise.

HYMN LXV. Common Metre.   *J.*
The Kingdom of God, not in word, but in power.

1 A Form of words tho' e'er so sound
  Can never save a soul,
The Holy Ghost must give the wound,
  And make the wounded whole.

2 Though GOD's election is a truth,
  Small comfort there I see,
'Till I am told by GOD's own mouth,
  That He has chosen me.

3 Sinners, I read, are justified,
  By faith in JESUS' blood:
But when to me that blood's appli'd,
  'Tis then I've peace with GOD.

4 Imputed righteousness I own,
  A doctrine most divine;
When JESUS to my heart makes known,
  That all his merit's mine.

5 To perseverance I agree;
  The thing to me is clear;
        Because

AFTER SERMON.

Because the LORD has promis'd me,
  That I shall persevere.

6 Thus christians glorify the LORD;
    His Spirit joins with ours,
  In bearing witness to his word,
    With all its saving pow'rs.

HYMN LXVI. Common Metre. Edm. Jones. J.
  The successful Resolve. Est. iv. 16.

1 COME, humble sinner, in whose
      breast,
    A thousand thoughts revolve,
  Come, with your guilt and fear opprest,
    And make this last resolve.

2 "I'll go to JESUS, tho' my sin
  " Hath like a mountain rose;
  " I know his courts, I'll enter in,
  " Whatever may oppose.

3 "Prostrate I'll lie before his throne,
  " And there my guilt confess,
  " I'll tell him I'm a wretch undone
  " Without his sovereign grace.

4 "I'll to the gracious King approach,
  " Whose sceptre pardon gives,
                            " Perhaps

  "Perhaps he may command my touch,
   "And then the suppliant lives.

5 "Perhaps he will admit my plea,
  "Perhaps will hear my prayer;
 "But if I perish I will pray,
  "And perish only there.

6 "I can but perish if I go,
  "I am resolv'd to try:
 For if I stay away, I know
  I must forever die."

HYMN LXVII. Common Metre. Ryland, Jun. *J.*
Hell the Sinners own Place.

1 LORD when I read the traitor's doom
  To "his own place" consign'd,
What holy humble fear and hope
  Alternate fill my mind!

2 Traitor to thee I too have been,
  But sav'd by matchless grace,
Or else the lowest, hottest hell
  Had surely been my place.

3 Thither I was by law adjudg'd,
  And thitherward rush'd on;
And there in my eternal doom
  Thy justice might have shone.

        4 But

4 But lo! (what wond'rous, matchless love)
    I call a place my own
On earth, within the gospel sound,
    And at thy gracious throne.

5 A place is mine among thy saints,
    A place at JESUS' feet,
And I expect in Heaven a place
    Where saints and angels meet.

6 Blest lamb of God, thy sovereign grace
    To all around I'd tell,
Which made a place in glory mine,
    Whose just desert was hell.

HYMN LXVIII. Common Metre.   J.
Dismission.

1 FATHER, before we hence depart
    Send thy good Spirit down;
Let him reside in every heart,
    And bless the seed that's sown.

2 Thou fountain of eternal love!
    Who gav'st thy Son to die;
O let thy Spirit from above,
    Enlighten and apply.

HYMN LXIX. Common Metre. Rippon's Col. J.

Dismission.

1 IN vain Apollo's silver tongue,
    And Paul's with strains profound,
Diffuse among the listening throng,
    The Gospel's glad'ning sound.

2 JESUS, the work is wholly thine,
    To form the heart anew,
Now let thy sovereign grace divine
    Each stubborn soul renew.

HYMN LXX. Common Metre. Dr. Watts. J.

The prospect of Heaven makes death easy

1 THERE is a land of pure delight,
    Where saints immortal reign:
Infinite day excludes the night,
    And pleasure banish pain.

2 There everlasting spring abides,
    And never fading flow'rs:
Death, like a narrow sea, divides
    This heav'nly land from ours.

3 [Sweet fields beyond the swelling flood,
    Stand dress'd in living green:
So to the Jews old Canaan stood,
    While Jordan roll'd between.

4 But

4 But fearful mortals start and shrink,
    To cross this narrow sea;
And linger, shiv'ring on the brink,
    And fear to launch away.]

5 O! Could we make our doubts remove
    Those gloomy doubts that rise,
And see the Canaan that we love,
    With unbeclouded eyes?

6 Could we but climb where Moses stood,
    And view the landskip o'er,
Not Jordan's streams, nor death's cold
Should fright us from the shore. (flood

HYMN LXXI.   Common Metre.   Rippon's Coll. J.
Sanctification Sought.

1 NOW may the GOD of peace & love
    Who from the imprisoning grave
Restor'd the Shepherd of the sheep,
    Omnipotent to save.

2 Thro' the rich Merits of that blood,
    Which he on Calvary spilt,
To make th' eternal Cov'nant sure,
    On which our hopes are built.

3 Perfect our souls in every grace,
    T' accomplish all his will,
                            And

And all that's pleasing in his sight,
  Inspire us to fulfil!

4 For the great Mediator's sake,
  We for these blessings pray:
With glory let his name be crown'd,
  Thro' Heaven's eternal day!

HYMN LXXII. Common Metre. Rippon's Coll. J.
Praise to the Lamb.

1 NOT unto us, but thee alone,
  Blest Lamb, be glory given!
Here shall thy praises be begun,
  And carried on in Heaven.

2 The host of spirits now with thee,
  Eternal anthems sing:
To imitate them here, lo! we,
  Our Hallelujahs bring.

3 Had we our tongues like them inspir'd,
  Like theirs our songs shou'd rise;
Like them we never should be tir'd,
  But love the sacrifice.

4 'Till we the veil of flesh lay down,
  Accept our weaker lays;

AFTER SERMON. 67

And when we reach thy father's throne
We'll give thee nobler praise.

HYMN LXXIII. Common Metre. Dr. Watts. J.
God our only happiness.

1 MY God, my portion, & my love
     My everlasting All;
  I've none but thee in Heav'n above,
     Or on this earthly ball.

2 What empty things are all the skies,
     And this inferior clod!
  There's nothing here deserves my joys,
     There's nothing like my God.

3 In vain the bright, the burning sun,
     Scatters his feeble light:
  'Tis thy sweet beams create my noon;
     If thou withdraw, 'tis night.

4 And whilst upon my restless bed,
     Amidst the shades I roll,
  If my Redeemer raise my head,
     'Tis morning with my soul.

5 To thee we owe our wealth and friends,
     And health, and safe abode:
  We praise thy name for all these things,
     But they are not our God.

6 Were

6 Were I possessor of the earth,
   And call'd the stars my own;
Without thy graces and thyself,
   I were a wretch undone.

HYMN LXXIV. Common Metre. *J.*
Desiring Assurance of God's favor.

1 ETERNAL source of joys divine,
   To thee my soul aspires:
O could I say, " The Lord is mine,"
   'Tis all my soul desires.

2 Thy smile can give me real joy,
   Unmingled, and refin'd;
Substantial bliss without alloy,
   And lasting as the mind.

3 Thy smiles can gild the shades of woe,
   Bid stormy trouble cease,
Spread the fair dawn of heav'n below,
   And sweeten pain to peace.

4 My hope, my trust, my life, my Lord,
   Assure me of thy love;
O speak the kind transporting word,
   And bid my fear remove.

5 Then

5 Then shall my thankful pow'rs rejoice,
 And triumph in my God,
Till heav'nly transport tunes my voice,
 To spread thy praise abroad.

HYMN LXXV. Common Metre. Dr. Watts. J.

Safety in God.

1 ARISE, my soul, my joyful pow'rs
 And triumph in my God;
Awake, my voice, and loud proclaim
 His glorious grace abroad.

2 He rais'd me from the deeps of sin,
 The gates of gaping hell,
And fix'd my standing more secure,
 Than 'twas before I fell.

3 The arms of everlasting love,
 Beneath my soul he plac'd,
And on the rock of ages set
 My slipp'ry footsteps fast.

4 The city of my bless'd abode
 Is wall'd around with grace;
Salvation for a bulwark stands
 To shield the sacred place.

5 Satan may vent his sharpest spite,
 And all his legions roar;

Almighty

Almighty mercy guards my life,
And bounds his raging pow'r.

6 Arise, my soul, awake, my voice,
And songs of praises sing;
Loud hallelujahs shall address
My Saviour and my King.

HYMN LXXVI. Common Metre.   J.
For New Year's Day.

1 AND now, my soul another year,
Of thy short life is past.
I cannot long continue here,
And this may be my last.

2 Much of my dubious life is gone,
Nor will return again;
And swift my passing moments run,
The few that yet remain.

3 Awake, my soul, with utmost care
Thy true condition learn;
What are thy hopes, how sure, how fair
And what thy great concern.

4 Now a new scene of time begins,
Set out afresh for Heaven;
Seek pardon for thy former sins,
In Christ so freely given.

5 Devoutly

5 Devoutly yield thyself to God,
 And on his grace depend;
With zeal pursue the heav'nly road,
 Nor doubt a happy end.

HYMN LXXVII. Common Metre. Dr. S. Stennett. J.

The Attraction of the Cross, (John xii. 32.)

1 YONDER--- amazing Sight!---I see
 Th' incarnate Son of GOD,
Expiring on the accursed tree,
 And welt'ring in his blood.

2 Behold a purple torrent run
 Down from his hands and head:
The crimson tide puts out the sun;
 His groans awake the dead.

3 The trembling earth, the darken'd sky
 Proclaim the truth aloud!
And with th' amaz'd centurion cry,
 " This is the son of God."

4 So great, so vast a sacrifice
 May well my hope revive:
If GOD's own Son thus bleeds and dies,
 The sinner sure may live.

5 O that these cords of love divine,
 Might draw me, Lord to thee,

Thou

Thou haſt my heart, it ſhall be thine--
Thine it ſhall ever be!

HYMN LXXVIII. Common Metre.   *A.*

Contrition.

1 O Thou whoſe tender mercy hears
    Contrition's humble ſigh;
  Whoſe hand indulgent wipes the tears
    From ſorrow's weeping eye.

2 See! low before thy throne of grace,
    We wretched wanderers mourn;
  Haſt thou not bid us ſeek thy face?
    Haſt thou not ſaid, return?

3 And ſhall our guilty fears prevail
    To drive us from thy feet?
  O let not this dear refuge fail,
    This only ſafe retreat.

4 O ſhine on this benighted heart
    With beams of mercy ſhine;
  And let thy healing voice impart
    A taſte of joys divine.

5 Thy preſence only can beſtow
    Delights which never cloy;
  Be this my ſolace here below,
    And my eternal joy.

HYMN

AFTER SERMON.

HYMN LXXIX. Common Metre. The Coll. A.
Providence.

1 GOD moves in a mysterious way,
    His wonders to perform;
He plants his footsteps in the sea,
    And rides upon the storm.

2 Deep in unfathomable mines
    Of never failing skill,
He treasures up his bright designs,
    And works his sovereign will.

3 Ye fearful saints fresh courage take;
    The clouds you so much dread
Are big with mercy and shall break
    In blessings on your head.

4 Judge not the Lord by feeble sense,
    But trust him for his grace;
Behind a frowning Providence
    He hides a smiling face.

5 His purposes will ripen fast,
    Unfolding every hour;
The bud may have a bitter taste
    But sweet will be the flow'r.

6 Blind unbelief is sure to err,
    And scan his work in vain:

God is his own interpreter,
And he will make it plain.

HYMN LXXX. Common Metre. The Coll. A.
Rapture.

1 From thee, my God, my joys shall rise
And run eternal rounds,
Beyond the limits of the skies,
And all created bounds.

2 The holy triumphs of my soul
Shall death itself outbrave,
Leave dull mortality behind,
And fly beyond the grave.

3 There where my blessed Jesus reigns,
In Heaven's unmeasur'd space,
I'll spend a long eternity
In pleasure and in praise.

4 Millions of years my wondering eyes
Shall o'er thy beauties rove,
And endless ages I'll adore,
The glories of thy love.

5 Sweet Jesus every smile of thine
Shall fresh endearments bring;
And thousand tastes of new delights,
From all thy graces spring.

HYMN

AFTER SERMON.

LXXXI. Common Metre. The Coll. A.
Christian Soldier.

1 DRESS uniform the soldier's wear,
　　When duty calls abroad;
Not purchas'd at their cost or care,
　　But by the prince bestowed.

2 Christ's soldiers too, if Christ-like bred,
　　Have regimental dress;
'Tis linen white, faced with red,
　　'Tis Christ's own righteousness.

3 A rich and sightly robe it is,
　　And to the soldier dear;
No rose can learn to blush like this,
　　Nor lily look so fair.

4 'Tis wrought by Jesus' skilful hand,
　　And ting'd with his own blood;
It make the Cherubs gazing stand
　　To view this robe of God.

5 This vesture never waxeth old,
　　Nor spot thereon can fall;
It makes a soldier brisk and bold,
　　And dutiful withall.

6 This robe put on me, Lord each day,
　　And it shall hide my shame,

Shall make me fight and sing and pray
And bless my captain's name.

HYMN LXXXII. Common Metre. The Coll. *A.*
General.

1 GLORY to GOD, who gave the word
    And bid the preachers cry;
Who caus'd his will to be proclaim'd,
    And brought salvation nigh.

2 LORD, ever give us of this bread,
    And grant us ears to hear;
Hearts to receive the heav'nly seed,
    And bring forth fruit with fear.

3 O may thy word direct our path,
    And guide our fault'ring feet;
Direct us in the living way,
    And to thy mercy seat!

4 Fill every hungry soul, that cries,
    From thine exhaustless store;
And let no one go empty hence,
    But taste, and pray for more.

5 Let all thy children, LORD, be fed,
    With the eternal word;
Be wise, and stronger grow thereby,
    Increasing in the LORD.

AFTER SERMON.

HYMN LXXXIII. Common Metre. Dr. Watts. *A.*

A Godly sorrow for Christ's sufferings.

1 ALAS! and did my Saviour bleed!
    And did my sov'reign die;
Wou'd he devote that sacred head
    For such a worm as I?

2 Was it for crimes that I had done,
    He groan'd upon the tree?
Amazing pity! grace unknown!
    And love beyond degree.

3 Well might the sun in darkness hide,
    And shut his glories in,
When Christ the mighty Saviour dy'd
    For man his creature's sin.

4 Thus might I hide my blushing face,
    While his dear cross appears,
Dissolve my heart in tenderness,
    And melt my eyes in tears.

5 But drops of grief can ne'er repay
    The debt of love I owe;
Here, Lord, I give myself away,
    'Tis all that I can do.

HYMN LXXXIV. Com. Metre. Dr. Doddridge. J.
Salvation Approaching.

1 AWAKE, ye saints, and lift your eyes
    And raise your voices high;
Awake, and praise that sovereign love
    That shews salvation nigh.

2 On all the wings of time it flies,
    Each moment brings it near:
Then welcome each declining day;
    And each revolving year!

3 Not many years their round shall run,
    Nor many mornings rise,
Ere all its glories stand reveal'd
    To our admiring eyes.

4 Ye wheels of nature, speed your course
    Ye mortal powers, decay;
Fast as ye bring the night of death,
    Ye bring eternal day.

HYMN LXXXV. Common Metre. Rippon's Coll. J.
The Parable of the Sower. Matt. xiii. 3—10.

1 NOW, Lord, the heav'nly seed is sown,
    Be it thy servant's care
Thy heavenly blessing to bring down,
    By humble fervent prayer.

2 In vain we plant without thine aid,
    And water too in vain;
  Lord of the harvest, God of grace,
    Send down thy heav'nly rain.

3 Then shall our chearful hearts & tongues
    Begin this song divine;
  "Thou, Lord, hast given the rich increase
  " And be the glory thine."

HYMN LXXXVI. Common Metre. The Coll. *J.*

1 O Jesu, Jesu, dearest Lord,
    How wond'rous is thy love!
  Thy patience, pity, tenderness,
    Which I each moment prove!

2 O Lord, how faithless is my heart,
    How apt to turn aside;
  And wander in its own deceits,
    Of reasoning and pride!

3 Yet, dearest Saviour, love me still,
    The poorest, and the worst;
  For well I know where sin abounds,
    Thy grace abounds the most.

4 Yet let me not thy grace abuse,
    And sin because thou'rt good;

But let thy love fill me with shame,
  That I thy love withstood.

5 On me, my King, exert thy pow'r,
  Make old things pass away,
Create all new, and draw me still,
  Still nearer ev'ry day.

6 I thank and praise thee, dearest LORD,
  For all that thou hast done:
O take me to thee as I am,
  For thy redeemed one.

LXXXVII. Common Metre. (Ps. lxxi) *J.*
Rejoicing in hope.

1 MY Saviour, my Almighty friend,
  When I begin to praise;
Where will the growing numbers end,
  The numbers of thy grace?

2 Thou art my everlasting trust,
  Thy goodness I adore!
Send down thy grace, O blessed LORD,
  That I may love thee more.

3 My feet shall travel all the length,
  Of the celestial road;
And march with courage in thy strength
  To see the LORD my GOD.

4 How will my lips rejoice to tell
    The vict'ries of my King!
My soul redeem'd from sin and hell,
    Shall thy salvation sing.

5 My tongue shall all the day proclaim,
    My Saviour and my GOD;
His death hath brought my foes to shame
    And drown'd them in his blood.

6 Awake, awake, my tuneful pow'rs,
    With this delightful song
I'll entertain the darkest hours,
    Nor think the season long.

HYMN LXXXVIII. Common Metre. Steel. *J.*
Praise to the Redeemer.

1 TO our Redeemer's glorious name
    Awake the sacred song!
O may his love (immortal flame)
    Tune ev'ry heart and tongue.

2 His love what mortal thought can reach
    What mortal tongue display?
Imagination's utmost stretch
    In wonder dies away.

Let wonder still with love unite,
   And gratitude and joy;
Jesus be our supreme delight,
   His praise our best employ.

Jesus, who left his throne on high,
   Left the bright realms of bliss,
And came to earth to bleed and die:—
   Was ever love like this?

Dear Lord, while we adoring pay,
   Our humble thanks to thee;
May ev'ry heart with rapture say,
   " The Saviour dy'd for me."

O may the sweet the blissful theme
   Fill ev'ry heart and tongue,
Till strangers love thy charming name,
   And join the sacred song.

HYMN LXXXIX. Common Metre.   Steel. J.

Watchfulness and Prayer. (Matt. xxvi. 41.)

ALAS, what hourly dangers rise!
   What snares beset my way!
To Heaven O let me lift my eyes,
   And hourly watch and pray.

How oft my mournful thoughts complain,
   And melt in flowing tears;

My weak refistance, ah! how vain!
  How ftrong my foes and fears.

3 O gracious GOD, in whom I live,
  My feeble efforts aid,
Help me to watch, and pray, and ftrive,
  Tho' trembling and afraid.

4 Increafe my faith, increafe my hope,
  When foes and fears prevail;
And bear my fainting fpirits up,
  Or foon my ftrength will fail.

5 When ere temptations fright my heart,
  Or lure my feet afide,
My GOD, thy powerful aid impart,
  My guardian and my guide.

6 O keep me in thy heavenly way,
  And bid the tempter flee;
And let me never, never ftray
  From happinefs and thee.

HYMN XC. Common Metre. The Coll. J.

The Sinner converted.

1 OFT I reflect upon thy grace,
    With tears of thankfulnefs,
  Which call'd me from my native place,
    The world's wide wildernefs.

2 My precious time I vainly spent,
  Subject to nature's sway;
 My corrupt, carnal will was bent
  Its motion to obey.

3 Thick darkness overspread my mind,
  I stumbled in the night,
 All my affections were inclin'd
  To creaturely delight.

4 God saw me in this wretched case,
  A slave to base desire;
 And, by an act of special grace,
  The brand pluck'd from the fire.

5 O may a sense of mercies past,
  Stir up my soul to praise;
 And whet my appetite to taste,
  Thy larger draughts of grace.

HYMN XCI. Common Metre. The Coll. J.

The Believer's Hope.

1 HE is a God of sov'reign love,
  That promis'd Heav'n to me;
 And taught my thoughts to soar above,
  Where happy spirits be.

2 Prepare me, Lord for thy right hand,
  Then come the joyful day!

Come

Come death and some celestial band !
  To bear my soul away.

3 Then, my beloved, take my soul
    Up to thy blest abode;
  That face to face I may behold
    My Saviour and my GOD.

4 GOD has laid up in Heav'n for me
    A crown which cannot fade;
  The righteous Judge at the great day
    Shall place it on my head.

5 Nor hath the King of grace decreed
    This prize for me alone;
  But all that love and long to see
    Th' appearance of his Son.

HYMN XCII. Common Metre. The Coll. *J.*
The Christian's Expectation.

1 GOD of all consolation, take
    The glory of thy grace;
  Thy gifts to thee we render back
    In ceaseless songs of praise.

2 Not unto us, but thee, O LORD,
    Glory to thee be giv'n,
  For ev'ry gracious thought and word,
    That brought us nearer Heav'n.

3 Our souls are in his mighty hand,
  And He will keep them still;
And you and I shall surely stand
  With Him on Zion's hill.

4 Him eye to eye we there shall see,
  Our face, like his, shall shine;
O what a glorious company,
  When saints and angels join!

5 O what a joyful meeting there,
  In robes of white array'd;
Palms in our hands we all shall bear,
  And crowns upon our head!

6 Then let us earnestly contend,
  And fight our passage thro';
Bear in our faithful mind the end,
  And keep the prize in view.

HYMN XCIII. Common Metre. The Coll. *J.*
Breathing after Heavenly Things.

1 TO thee, my GOD, I hourly sigh,
  But not for golden stores;
Nor covet I the brightest gems,
  On the rich eastern shores.

2 Nor that deluding empty joy,
  Men call a mighty name;

Nor

Nor greatness in its gayest forms,
 My restless thoughts enflame.

3 Nor pleasure's soft enticing charms,
 My fond desires allure;
Far greater things than earth can yield,
 My wishes would secure.

4 Those blissful, those transporting smiles,
 That brighten Heav'n above;
The boundless riches of thy grace,
 And treasures of thy love.

5 These are the mighty things I crave:
 O! make these blessings mine;
And all the glories of the world
 I gladly will resign.

HYMN XCIV. Common Metre. The Coll. J. *Tribulation.*

1 THE souls that would to JESUS press
 Must fix this firm and sure,
That tribulation, more or less,
 They must and shall endure.

2 From this there can be none exempt;
 'Tis GOD's own wise decree:
Satan the weakest saint will tempt,
 Nor is the stongest free.

3 The world opposes from without,
    And unbelief within:
  We fear, we faint, we grieve, we doubt,
    And feel the load of sin.

4 Glad frames too often lift us up,
    And then how proud we grow,
  'Till sad desertion makes us droop,
    And down we sink as low.

5 Ten thousand baits the foe prepares
    To catch the wand'ring heart;
  And seldom do we see the snares,
    Before we feel the smart.

6 But let not all this terrify;
    Pursue the narrow path;
  Look to the LORD with stedfast eye,
    And fight with hell by faith.

7 Tho' we are feeble, CHRIST is strong;
    His promises are true;
  We shall be conqu'rors all ere long,
    And more than conqu'rors too.

HYMN XCV. Common Metre. Dr. Watts. J.
Trials overcome by Hope.

1 WHEN I can read my title clear,
    To mansions in the skies,

I bid farewell to ev'ry fear,
   And wipe my weeping eyes.

2 Should earth against my soul engage,
   And hellish darts be hurl'd,
Then I can smile at satan's rage,
   And face a frowning world.

3 Let cares like a wild deluge come,
   And storms of sorrow fall;
May I but safely reach my home.
   My God, my Heav'n, my All:

4 There shall I bathe my weary soul
   In seas of heav'nly rest,
And not a wave of trouble roll
   Across my peaceful breast.

HYMN XCVI. *Common Metre.* Dr. Watts. J.

1 NAKED as from the earth we came
      And crept to life at first,
   We to the earth return again,
      And mingle with our dust.

2 The dear delights we here enjoy,
      And fondly call our own,
   Are but short favours borrow'd now,
      To be repaid anon.

3 'Tis God that lifts our comforts high,
    Or sinks them in the grave,
  He gives, and (blessed be his name!)
    He takes but what he gave.

4 Peace all our angry passions then,
    Let each rebellious sigh
  Be silent at his sov'reign will,
    And every murmur die.

5 If smiling mercy crown our lives,
    Its praises shall be spread,
  And we'll adore the justice too
    That strikes our comforts dead.

HYMN XCVII. Com. Metre. Dr. Watts Serm. 7.
Holy Fortitude.

1 AM I a soldier of the cross?
    A follower of the Lamb?
  And shall I fear to own his cause?
    Or blush to speak his name?

2 Must I be carry'd to the skies,
    On flowery beds of ease,
  While others fought to win the prize,
    And sail'd through bloody seas?

3 Are there no foes for me to face?
    Must I not stem the flood?

AFTER SERMON.

    Is this vile world a friend to grace,
      To help me on to GOD?

4 Sure I must fight if I would reign;
    Increase my courage LORD:
  I'll bear the cross, endure the pain,
    Supported by thy word.

5 Thy saints, in all this glorious war,
    Shall conquer though they die;
  They see the triumph from afar,
    And seize it with their eye.

6 When that illustrious day shall rise,
    And all thy armies shine,
  In robes of vict'ry through the skies,
    The glory shall be thine.

HYMN XCVIII. Common Metre. Dr. Watts. *J.*

Invitation.

1 LET ev'ry mortal ear attend,
    And ev'ry heart rejoice;
  The trumpet of the gospel sounds
    With an inviting voice.

2 Come all ye hungry starving souls
    That feed upon the wind,
  And vainly strive with earthly toys
    To fill an empty mind;

              3 Eternal

3 Eternal wisdom has prepar'd
    A soul reviving feast,
And bids your longing appetites
    The rich provision taste.

4 Ho! ye that pant for living streams,
    And pine away and die;
Here you may quench your raging thirst
    With springs that never dry.

5 Rivers of love and mercy here,
    In a rich ocean join;
Salvation in abundance flows,
    Like floods of milk and wine.

XCIX. Common Metre. (Psi. Dr. Watts.) *J.*
The way and end of the righteous and wicked.

1 BLEST is the man, who shuns the place
    Where sinners love to meet;
Who fears to tread their wicked ways,
    And hates the scoffer's seat.

2 But in the statutes of the Lord,
    Has plac'd his chief delight;
By day he reads or hears the word,
    And meditates by night.

3 Green as the leaf and ever fair,
    Shall his profession shine;

While

While fruits of holiness appear
　　　　Like clusters on the vine.

4 Not so the impious and unjust;
　　　What vain designs they form!
　Their hopes are blown away like dust,
　　　Or chaff before the storm.

5 Sinners in judgment shall not stand,
　　　Amongst the sons of grace,
　When Christ the judge at his right hand
　　　Appoints his saints a place.

6 His eye beholds the path they tread,
　　　His heart approves it well;
　But crooked ways of sinners lead,
　　　Down to the gates of hell.

　　　HYMN C. Common Metre. The Col. J.
　　　　　A prayer for faith.

1 FATHER, I stretch my hands to thee
　　　No other help I know;
　If thou withdraw thyself from me,
　　　Ah! whither shall I go?

2 What did thine only Son endure,
　　　Before I drew my breath?
　What pain, what labour, to secure,
　　　My soul from endless death!

3 O Jesus, could I thus believe,
　　I now should feel thy pow'r;
　Now my poor soul thou would'st receive
　　Nor let me wait one hour.

4 Author of faith, to thee I lift
　　My weary, longing eyes;
　O let me now receive that gift!
　　My soul without it dies!

HYMN CI. Com. Metre. Dr. Watts. Zech. xiii 1. J.

1 HOW sad our state by nature is!
　　Our sin, how deep it stains!
　And satan binds our captive souls
　　Fast in his slavish chains.

2 But there's a voice of sov'reign grace
　　Sounds from God's sacred word;
　" Ho! ye despairing sinners, come,
　" And trust upon the Lord."

3 O may we hear th' Almighty call,
　　And run to this relief;
　We would believe thy promise, Lord,
　　O! help our unbelief.

4 To the blest fountain of thy blood,
　　Teach us, O Lord! to fly:

　　　　　　　　　　　There

There may we wash our spotted souls
From crimes of deepest dye!

5 Stretch out thine arm, victorious King,
Our reigning sins subdue,
Drive the old dragon from his seat,
And form our souls anew.

6 Poor, guilty, weak and helpless worms,
On thy kind arm we fall;
Be thou our strength and righteousness
Our JESUS and our All.

HYMN CII. Common Metre. The Coll. *J.*
Renewing Grace.

1 JESU Redeemer, Saviour, Lord,
The weary sinner's friend;
Come to my help, pronounce the word,
Bid my corruptions end.

2 Thou canst o'ercome this heart of mine,
Thou canst victorious prove,
For everlasting strength is thine,
And everlasting love.

3 Thy powerful spirit can subdue
Unconquerable sin,
Cleanse my foul heart and make it clean
And write thy law within.

4 Speak

4 Speak and the deaf shall hear thy voice
 The blind his sight receive,
 The dumb in songs of praise rejoice,
 The heart of stone believe.

5 The Æthiop then shall change his skin,
 The dead shall feel thy power;
 The loathsome leper shall be clean,
 And I shall sin abhor.

HYMN CIII. Long Metre. The Coll.   J.
The pressure of sin.

1 O That my load of sin were gone!
 O that I could at last submit,
 At Jesus' feet to lay me down,
 To lay my soul at Jesus' feet!

2 When shall mine eyes behold the Lamb,
 The GOD of my salvation see!
 Weary, O LORD, thou know'st I am;
 Yet still I cannot come to thee.

3 Rest for my soul I long to find;
 Saviour, if mine indeed thou art,
 Give me thy meek and lowly mind,
 And stamp thine image on my heart.

4 I would, but thou must give the pow'r,
 My heart from ev'ry sin release;
 Bring

AFTER SERMON.

 Bring near, bring near the joyful hour,
  And fill me with thy heav'nly peace.

5 Come, LORD, the drooping sinner chear
  Let not my JESUS long delay;
 Appear, in my hard heart appear,
  My GOD, my Saviour, come away.

CIV. Common Metre. (Pf. 51.) *J.*

1 LORD, I would spread my sore distress
  And guilt before thine eyes;
 Against thy law, against thy grace,
  How high my crimes arise!

2 I from the stock of Adam came,
  Unholy and unclean;
 All my original is shame,
  And all my nature sin.

3 Born in a world of guilt, I drew,
  Contagion with my breath;
 And as my days advanc'd I grew,
  A juster prey for death.

4 Cleanse me, O LORD, and chear my soul
  With thy forgiving love;
 O make my broken spirit whole,
  And bid my sins remove.

5 Let not thy spirit quite depart,
    Nor drive me from thy face;
Create anew my vicious heart
    And fill it with thy grace.

6 Then shall I make thy mercy known,
    Before the sons of men;
Backsliders shall address thy throne,
    And turn to God again.

CV. Common Metre. (Pf. 126.)   J.
The joy of Conversion.

When God reveal'd his gracious name
    And chang'd my mournful state,
My rapture seem'd a pleasing dream,
    The grace appear'd so great.

2 The world beheld the glorious change,
    And did thy hand confess:
My tongue broke out in unknown strains
    And sung surprising grace.

3 Great is the work, my neighbours cry'd
    And own'd the pow'r divine;
Great is the work, my heart reply'd,
    And be the glory thine.

4 The Lord can clear the darkest skies,
    Can give us day for night,

Make drops of sacred sorrows rise,
    To rivers of delight.

5 Let those that sow in sadness wait,
    'Till the fair harvest come;
They shall confess their sheaves are great
    And shout the blessings home.

6 Tho' seed lie buried long in dust,
    It shan't deceive their hope!
The precious grain can ne'er be lost,
    For grace insures the crop.

HYMN CVI. Common Metre. Dr. Watts. J.
A Living and Dead Faith.

1 Mistaken souls! that dream of Heav'n
    And make their empty boast
Of inward joys and sins forgiv'n,
    While they are slaves to lust!

2 Vain are our fancies, airy flights,
    If faith be cold and dead;
None but a living pow'r unites,
    To Christ the living head.

3 'Tis faith that changes all the hearts;
    'Tis faith that works by love;
That bids all sinful joys depart,
    And lifts the thoughts above.

4 'Tis faith that conquers earth and hell
    By a celestial pow'r;
This is the grace that shall prevail
    In the decisive hour.

HYMN CVII. Common Metre. The Coll. J.
Ezekiel xxxvi. 26.

1 ALMIGHTY GOD of truth and love
    In me thy pow'r exert;
The mountain from my soul remove,
    The hardness of my heart:
My most obdurate heart subdue,
    In honor to thy Son,
And now the gracious wonder shew,
    And take away the stone.

2 I want a principle within,
    Of jealous, godly fear;
A sensibility of sin,
    A pain to feel it near:
I want the first approach to feel
    Of pride, or vain desire,
To catch the wand'rings of my will,
    And quench the kindling fire.

3 From thee that I no more depart,
    No more thy goodness grieve;

The filial awe, the fleshly heart,
  The tender conscience give:
Quick as the apple of an eye,
  O God! my conscience make:
Awake my soul when sin is nigh,
  And keep it still awake.

HYMN CVIII. Common Metre. The Coll.   J.
The Heavenly guest. Rev. iii. 20.

1 AND will the Lord thus condescend
    To visit sinful worms?
  Thus at the door shall mercy stand,
    In all her winning forms?

2 Surprizing grace!---and shall my heart
    Unmov'd and cold remain?
  Has this hard rock no tender part?
    Must mercy plead in vain?

3 Shall Jesus for admission sue,
    His charming voice unheard?
  And this vile heart, his rightful due,
    Remain for ever barr'd?

4 'Tis sin, alas! with tyrant power
    The lodging has possess'd;
  And crouds of traitors bar the door
    Against the heav'nly guest.

5 Lord

5 Lord, rise in thy all conqu'ring grace,
  Thy mighty power display;
One beam of glory from thy face
  Can drive my foes away.

6 Ye dangerous inmates, hence depart;
  Dear Saviour enter in,
And guard the passage of my heart,
  And keep out ev'ry sin.

HYMN CIX. Common Metre. Dr. Watts J.

Weakness Bewailed.

1 WHY is my heart so far from thee
    My God, my chief delight?
  Why are my thoughts no more by day,
    With thee, no more by night?

2 Why should my foolish passions rove?
    Where can such sweetness be,
  As I have tasted in thy love,
    As I have found in thee?

3 When my forgetful soul renews
    The favour of thy grace,
  My heart presumes I cannot lose
    The relish all my days.

4 But e'er one fleeting hour is past,
    The flatt'ring world employs

Some sensual bait to seize my taste,
  And to pollute my joys.

5 Then I repent and vex my soul,
  That I shou'd leave thee so:
  Where will those wild affections roll,
  That let a Saviour go?

CX. Common Metre. (Pf. ii. Dr. Watts.) J.
The Kingdom of Christ.

1 WHY did the nations join to slay
    The LORD's anointed Son?
  Why did they cast his laws away,
    And tread his gospel down?

2 The LORD that sits above the skies,
    Derides their rage below,
  He speaks with vengeance in his eyes,
    And strikes their spirits through.

3 "I call him my eternal Son,
  "And raise him from the dead;
  "I make my holy hill his throne,
    And will his kingdom spread.

4 "Ask me, my Son, and then enjoy,
  "The utmost heathen lands:
  "Thy rod of iron shall destroy
  "The rebel that withstands."

5 Be wife, ye rulers of the earth,
   Obey th' anointed LORD,
Adore the King of heav'nly birth,
   And tremble at his word.

6 With humble love addrefs his throne;
   For if he frown, ye die:
Thofe are fecure, and thofe alone
   Who on his grace rely.

CXI. Common Metre.   (Pf. 27.)   J.
Prayer and Hope.

1 SOON as I heard my father fay,
   " Ye children, feek my grace"
My heart reply'd without delay,
   I'll feek my father's face."

2 Let not thy face be hid from me,
   Nor frown my foul away:
GOD of my life, I fly to thee,
   In a diftreffing day.

3 Should friends and kindred near and dear
   Leave me to want or die,
My GOD would make my life his care,
   And all my need fupply.

4 My fainting flefh had dy'd with grief,
   Had not my foul believ'd,

                        To

To see thy grace provide relief,
  Nor was my hope deceiv'd.

Wait on the LORD, ye trembling saints,
  And keep your courage up,
He'll raise your spirit when it faints,
  And far exceed your hope.

HYMN CXII. Common Metre. Dr. Watts J.
Complaint of spiritual sloth.

MY drowsy pow'rs, why sleep ye so
  Awake, my sluggish soul!
Nothing has half thy work to do,
  Yet nothing's half so dull.

The little ants for one poor grain
  Labour, and tug, and strive;
Yet we, who have a heav'n t'obtain,
  How negligent we live!

We, for whose sake all nature stands,
  And stars their courses move;
We, for whose guard the angel-bands,
  Come flying from above:

We, for whom God the Son came down
  And labour'd for our good,
How careless to secure that crown
  He purchas'd with his blood!

5 Lord,

5 Lord, shall we lie so sluggish still,
  And never act our parts!
 Come, holy Dove, from th' heav'nly hill
  And sit and warm our hearts.

6 Then shall our active spirits move,
  Upward our souls shall rise;
 With hands of faith and wings of love,
  We'll fly and take the prize.

HYMN CXIII. Common Metre. Dr. Watts J.
Different success of the gospel.

1 CHRIST and his cross is all our theme
  The mist'ries that we speak,
 Are scandal in the Jews esteem,
  And folly to the Greek.

2 But souls enlighten'd from above
  With joy receive the word;
 They see what wisdom, pow'r, and love,
  Shines in their dying LORD.

3 The vital savour of his name
  Restores their fainting breath;
 But unbelief perverts the same,
  To guilt, despair, and death.

4 Till God diffuse his graces down,
  Like show'rs of heav'nly rain,

In

In vain Apollos sows the ground,
  And Paul may plant in vain.

HYMN CXIV. Common Metre. (Dr. Watts.) *A.*

A Sympathising Saviour.

1 With joy we meditate the grace
    Of our High Priest above;
  His heart is made of tenderness,
    His bowels melt with love.

2 Touch'd with a sympathy within,
    He knows our feeble frame;
  He knows what sore temptations mean,
    For he has felt the same.

3 He in the days of feeble flesh
    Pour'd out his cries and tears,
  And in his measure feels afresh,
    What ev'ry member bears.

4 He'll never quench the smoking flax,
    But raise it to a flame;
  The bruised reed he never breaks,
    Nor scorns the meanest name.

5 Then let our humble faith address
    His mercy and his pow'r,
  We shall obtain deliv'ring grace
    In the distressing hour.

HYMN CXV. Common Metre. Dr. Watts. A.
Deadness under the Word.

1 LONG have I sat beneath the sound
    Of thy salvation, LORD;
But still how weak my faith is found,
    And knowledge of thy word!

2 Oft I frequent thy holy place,
    And hear almost in vain:
How small a portion of thy grace
    My mem'ry can retain!

3 How cold and feeble is my love!
    How negligent my fear!
How low my hope of joys above!
    How few affections there!

4 Great GOD! thy sov'reign pow'r impart
    To give thy word success;
Write thy salvation in my heart,
    And make me learn thy grace.

5 Shew my forgetful feet the way
    That leads to joys on high,
There knowledge grows without decay,
    And love shall never die.

HYMN CXVI. Common Metre. Dr. Watts. *A.*
Flesh and Spirit.

What diff'rent pow'rs of grace & sin,
 Attend our mortal state?
I hate the thoughts that work within,
 And do the works I hate.

2 Now I complain, and groan, and die,
 While sin and satan reign:
Now raise my songs of triumph high,
 For grace prevails again.

3 So darkness struggles with the light,
 'Till perfect day arise;
Water and fire, maintain the fight,
 Until the weaker dies.

4 Thus will the flesh and spirit strive,
 And vex and break my peace;
But I shall quit this mortal life,
 And sin forever cease.

HYMN. CXVII. Common Metre Dr. Watts. *A.*
Justification by Christ only.

1 VAIN are the hopes the sons of men
 On their own works have built;
Their hearts by nature are unclean,
 And all their actions guilt.

D 2   Let

AFTER SERMON.

2 Let Jew and Gentile stop their mouths,
  Without a murm'ring word,
And the whole race of Adam stand
  Guilty before the Lord.

3 In vain we ask God's righteous law,
  To justify us now,
Since to convince and to condemn,
  Is all the law can do.

4 Jesus, how glorious is thy grace!
  When in thy name we trust,
Our faith receives a righteousness,
  That makes the sinner just.

HYMN CXVIII. Common Metre. Hart. *A.*
Perseverance.

1 THE sinner that by precious faith,
  Has felt his sins forgiv'n,
Is from that moment pass'd from death,
  And seal'd an heir of Heaven.

2 Tho' thousand snares enclose his feet,
  Not one shall hold him fast,
Whatever dangers he may meet,
  He shall get safe at last.

Not as the world the Saviour gives,
  He is no fickle friend:

Whom

Whom once he loves, he never leaves;
  But loves him to the end.

4 For Christ in ev'ry age has prov'd
    His purchase firm and true,
  If this foundation be remov'd,
    What shall the righteous do?

5 Brethren, by this your claim abide,
    This title to your bliss:
  Whatever loss you bear beside,
    O! never give up this.

HYMN CXIX. Common Metre. Dr. Watts. A.
         Repentance.

1 OH! if my soul was form'd for woe
    How would I vent my sighs!
  Repentance should like rivers flow,
    From both my streaming eyes.

2 'Twas for my sins, my dearest Lord,
    Hung on the cursed tree,
    And groan'd away a dying life,
  For thee, my soul, for thee.

3 O, how I hate those lusts of mine,
    That crucify'd my GOD;
  Those sins that pierc'd and nail'd his flesh
    Fast to the fatal wood!

                4 Yes

4 Yes, my Redeemer, they shall die,
    My heart hath so decreed;
  Nor will I spare those guilty things,
    That made my Saviour bleed.

5 Whilst with a melting broken heart,
    My murder'd LORD I view,
  I'll raise revenge against my sins,
    And slay the murd'rers too.

HYMN CXX. Common Metre. The Coll. A.
Petition.

1 O Dearest LORD, give me an heart
    Inflam'd with love to thee;
  That thro' thy tedious toil and smart,
    My soul may happy be.

2 I want, O LORD, from sin to flee,
    And in thy wounds to rest;
  Bid me by faith come near to thee.
    And lean upon thy breast.

3 Still let a sense of what thou'st done,
    In my hard heart be felt;
  That by the love to me thou'st shewn,
    My inmost soul may melt.

4 O may I never, never faint,
    Refresh'd by streams of love;

Till

AFTER SERMON.

Till in thy glory, as a saint,
I live with those above.

5 O may I now my all give up,
To thee my dearest LORD;
And wait with all thy saints to sup
Around the festal board.

HYMN CXXI. Common Metre. The Coll. A.
The Christian happy.

1 HOW happy is the christian's state,
His sins are all forgiv'n;
A chearing ray confirms the grace,
And lifts his hopes to heav'n.

2 Tho' in the rugged paths of life,
He heaves the pensive sigh;
Yet, trusting in his GOD, he finds,
Deliv'ring grace is nigh.

3 If, to prevent his wand'ring steps,
He feels the chast'ning rod;
The gentle stroke shall bring him back
To his forgiving GOD.

4 And when the welcome message comes,
To call his soul away;
His soul, in raptures, shall ascend,
To everlasting day.

AFTER SERMON.

HYMN CXXII. Long Metre. The Coll. *A.*
Sense of Pardon desired.

1 THY presence, Saviour, may I feel,
O stamp me with thy Spirit's seal
Lord, seal my pardon with thy blood,
And let me know I'm born of God.

2 One precious drop, Lord Jesus, grant
O! for one precious drop I pant!
By faith apply thy healing blood,
That I may cry, My Lord, my God.

3 Sprinkle it on my conscience, Lord,
O let me hear the pow'rful word,
That rais'd the dead, and chears the soul,
And makes the sin-sick sinner whole.

4 And when this mortal life is o'er,
And pain and sinning is no more,
Receive my soul to thy bless'd home:
O come, Lord Jesus, quickly come!

HYMN CXXIII. Long Metre. The Coll. *J.*
Preparing for Death.

1 OFT as the bell with solemn toll
Speaks the departure of a soul,
Let each one ask himself, am I
Prepar'd, should I be call'd to die!

2 Only

2 Only this frail and fleeting breath,
   Preserves me from the jaws of death;
   Soon as it fails, at once I'm gone,
   And plung'd into a world unknown.

3 Then leaving all I love below,
   To God's tribunal I must go;
   Must hear the judge pronounce my fate,
   And fix my everlasting state.

4 But could I bear to hear him say,
   " Depart, accursed, far away;
   With devils in the lowest hell
   Thou art forever doom'd to dwell.

5 Lord-Jesus! help me now to flee,
   And seek my hope alone in thee;
   Apply thy blood, thy spirit give,
   Subdue my sins, and in me live.

6 Then when the solemn bell I hear,
   If sav'd from guilt, I need not fear,
   Nor would the thought distressing be,
   Perhaps it next may toll for me.

7 Rather my spirits would rejoice,
   And wait impatient for thy voice;
   Glad when it bids me earth resign,
   Secure of heaven, if thou art mine.

D 4   HYMN

HYMN CXXIV. Long Metre. Addison. *J*.
The Heaven declare the Glory of God.

1 THE spacious Firmament on high,
   With all the blue, etherial sky,
And spangled heav'ns a shining flame,
Their great original proclaim.

2 Th' unweary'd sun from day to day,
Does his creator's pow'r display,
And publishes to ev'ry land;
The work of an Almighty hand.

3 Soon as the ev'ning shades prevail,
The moon takes up the wondrous tale,
And nightly to the list'ning earth,
Repeats the story of her birth.

4 While all the stars that round her burn,
And all the planets in their turn,
Confirm the tidings as they roll,
And spread the truth from pole to pole.

5 What though in solemn silence all
Move round this dark terrestrial ball?
What though no real voice nor sound,
Amidst their radiant orbs be found?

6 In reason's ear they all rejoice,
And utter forth a glorious voice,

For

AFTER SERMON.

For ever finging, as they fhine,
" The hand that made us is divine."

CXXV Long Metre. (Pf. lvii.)   *J.*
Protection and grace.

MY God, in whom are all the springs
  Of boundless love & grace unknown
Hide me beneath thy spreading wings,
  'Till the dark cloud is overblown.

2 Up to the heav'ns I send my cry,
  The Lord will my defires perform;
He fends his angel from the fky, (ftorm.
  And faves me from the threat'ning

3 Be thou exalted, O my GOD,
  Above the Heav'ns where angels dwell
Thy power on earth be known abroad,
  And land to land thy wonders tell.

4 My heart is fix'd; my fong fhall raife,
  Immortal honours to thy name;
Awake, my tongue, to found his praife
  My tongue, the glory of my frame

5 High o'er the earth his mercy reigns,
  And reaches to the utmoft fky;
His truth to endlefs years remains,
  When lower worlds diffolve and die.

6 Be thou exalted, O my God,
    Above the heav'ns where angels dwell
Thy pow'r on earth be known abroad,
    And land to land thy wonders tell.

CXXVI. Long Metre. (Pf. lxxv.)   *J.*
Mercy and truth met.

1 SALVATION is for ever nigh,
    The souls that fear & trust th' Lord,
And grace descending from on high,
    Fresh hopes of glory shall afford.

2 Mercy and truth on earth are met,
Since Christ the Lord came down from
By his obedience so complete, (heav'n?
Justice is pleas'd, and peace is giv'n.

3 Now truth and honour shall abound,
    Religion dwell on earth again,
And heav'nly influence bless the ground,
    In our Redeemer's gentle reign.

4 His righteousness is gone before,
    To give us free access to God:
Our wand'ring feet shall stray no more,
    But mark his steps and keep the road.

HYMN

AFTER SERMON.

HYMN CXXVII. Long Metre. Lyric Poems. A.
A dying Saviour.

1 HE dies! the heav'nly lover dies!
    The tidings strike a doleful sound
On my poor heart-strings: deep he lies,
    In the cold caverns of the ground.

2 Come saints, and drop a tear or two,
    On the dear bosom of your GOD,
He shed a thousand drops for you,
    A thousand drops of richer blood.

3 Here's love and grief beyond degree,
    The LORD of glory dies for men!
But lo, what sudden joys I see!
    JESUS the dead revives again.

4 Break off your tears, ye saints, and tell
    How high our great deliverer reigns;
Sing how he spoil'd the hosts of hell,
    And led the monster death in chains.

5 Say, live for ever wondrous King!
    Born to redeem, and strong to save!
Then ask the monster, where's his sting,
And where's thy victory, boasting grave?

HYMN CXXVIII. Long Metre. Steele.
Pardon and Rest for the weary Soul.

1 COME, weary souls with sin distrest,
   Come and accept the promis'd rest,
   The Saviour's gracious call obey,
   And cast your gloomy fears away.

2 Oppress'd with guilt, a painful load,
   O come, and spread your woes abroad,
   Divine compassion, mighty love,
   Will all the painful load remove.

3 Here mercy's boundless ocean flows,
   To cleanse your guilt and heal your woes,
   Pardon and life, and endless peace;
   How rich the gift! how free the grace.

4 Lord we accept with thankful hearts;
   The hope thy gracious word imparts;
   We come with trembling yet rejoice,
   And bless the kind inviting voice.

5 Dear Saviour! let thy powerful love,
   Confirm our faith, our fears remove;
   And sweetly influ'nce every breast,
   And guide us to eternal rest.

AFTER SERMON.

HYMN CXXIX. Long Metre. Doddridge. *1.*

Chufing the better part.

1 BESET with fnares on every hand,
In life's uncertain path I ftand:
Saviour divine, diffuse thy light,
To guide my doubtful footfteps right.

2 Engage this roving treacherous heart,
To fix on Mary's better part;
To fcorn the trifles of a day,
For joys, that none can take away.

3 Then let the wildeft ftorms arife:
Let tempefts mingle earth and fkies;
No fatal fhipwreck fhall I fear,
But all my treafures with me bear.

4 If thou, my JESUS, ftill be nigh,
Cheerful I live, and joyful die;
Secure, when mortal comforts flee,
To find ten thoufand worlds in thee.

HYMN CXXX. Long Metre. Lyric Poems. *A.*

Love to God.

1 OF all the joys we mortals know,
Jesus, thy love exceeds the reft;
Love, the beft bleffing here below,
The neareft image of the bleft.

2 While we are held in thy embrace,
   There's not a thought attempts to rove
Each smile upon thy beauteous face,
   Fixes, and charms, and fires our love.

3 While of thy absence we complain,
   And long, or weep in all we do,
There's a strange pleasure in the pain,
   And tears have their own sweetness too.

4 When round thy courts by day we rove,
   Or ask the watchman of the night,
For some kind tidings of our love,
   Thy very name creates delight.

5 Jesus, our God; yet rather come;
   Our eyes would dwell upon thy face,
'Tis best to see our Lord at home,
   And feel the presence of his grace.

CXXXI. Long Metre. (Pf. xxiv.)   *A.*
Saints dwell in Heaven.

1 THIS spacious earth is all the Lord's
      And men & worms & beasts & birds
   He rais'd the building on the seas,
      And gave it for their dwelling place.

2 But there's a brighter world on high,
      Thy palace, Lord, above the sky;
                                Who

AFTER SERMON.

Who shall ascend that blest abode,
    And dwell so near his maker GOD.

3 He that abhors and fears to sin, (clean
    Whose heart is pure, whose hands are
Him shall the LORD, the Saviour bless,
    And clothe his soul with right'ousness.

4 These are the men, the pious race
    That seek the God of Jacob's face;
These shall enjoy the blisful sight,
    And dwell in everlasting light.

CXXXII. Long Metre. (Ps. xxxii.)   A.
    Pardon.

1 BLess'd is the man, forever bless'd,
    Whose guilt is pardon'd by his GOD,
Whose sins with sorrow are confess'd,
    And cover'd with his Saviour's blood.

2 Bless'd is the man to whom the Lord
    Imputes not his iniquities,
He pleads no merit of reward,
    And not on works, but grace relies.

3 From guile his heart and lips are free,
    His humble joy his holy fear
With deep repentance well agree,
    And join to prove his faith sincere.

4 How glorious is that righteousness
    That blots and cancels all his sins!
While a bright evidence of grace
    Thro' his whole life appears and shines.

HYMN CXXXIII. Long Metre. Dr. Watts. *A.*
Misimprovement of Time.

1 HOW short and hasty is our life!
    How vast our soul's affairs!
Yet senseless mortals vainly strive,
    To lavish out their years.

2 Our days run thoughtlessly along,
    Without a moment's stay:
Just like a story or a song,
    We pass our lives away.

3 God from on high invites us home,
    But we march heedless on,
And ever hast'ning to the tomb,
    Stoop downwards as we run.

4 How we deserve the deepest hell,
    That slight the joys above!
What chains of vengeance should we (feel,
    That break such cords of love.

5 Draw us O God, with sov'reign grace,
    And lift our thoughts on high,
                  That

That we may end this mortal race,
And see salvation nigh.

HYMN CXXXIV. Long Metre. Dr. Watts. A.
Glory and Grace in the person of Christ.

1 NOW to the Lord, a noble song;
  Awake, my soul; awake, my tongue,
  Hosanna to th' eternal name,
  And all his boundless love proclaim.

2 See where it shines in JESUS' face,
  The brightest image of his grace;
  GOD, in the person of his Son,
  Has all his mightiest works outdone.

3 Yes, in his looks a glory stands,
  The noblest labour of thine hands;
  The pleasing lustre of his eyes,
  Outshines the wonders of the skies.

4 Grace! 'tis a sweet, a charming theme;
  My thoughts rejoice at JESUS' name!
  Ye angels, dwell upon the sound;
  Ye heav'ns reflect it to the ground!

5 O, may I live to see the place,
  Where he unveils his lovely face!
  Where all his beauties you behold,
  And sing his name on harps of gold.

AFTER SERMON.

HYMN CXXXV. Long Metre. Dr. Watts. A.
Desiring the divine presence.

1 WE are a garden wall'd around,
　　Chosen & made peculiar ground,
A little spot enclos'd by grace
Out of the world's wide wilderness.

2 Like trees of myrrh and spice we stand,
Planted by God the Father's hand;
And all his springs in Zion flow
To make this young plantation grow.

3 Awake, O heavenly wind, and come,
Blow on this garden of perfume;
Spirit divine, descend and breathe,
A gracious gale on plants beneath.

4 Make our best spices flow abroad
To entertain our Saviour God,
And faith and love and joy appear,
And every grace be active here.

HYMN CXXXVI. Long Metre. The Coll. A.
Confidence.

With all my pow'rs of heart & tongue,
　　I'll praise my maker with my song
Angels shall bear the notes I raise,
Approve the song, and join the praise.

2 I'll

AFTER SERMON.

2 I'll sing thy truth and mercy, LORD;
I'll sing the wonders of thy word;
Not all thy works, and names below,
So much thy pow'r and glory shew.

3 To GOD I cry'd when trouble rose;
He heard me, and subdu'd my foes;
He did my rising fears controul,
And strength diffus'd thro' all my soul.

4 Amidst a thousand snares I stand,
Upheld, and guarded by thy hand;
Thy words my fainting soul revive,
And keep my dying faith alive.

5 Grace will compleat what grace begins,
To save from sorrow, or from sins:
The work that wisdom undertakes,
Eternal mercy ne'er forsakes.

HYMN CXXXVII. Long Metre. The Coll. *A.*
Compleatness of Christ.

1 KIND is the speech of Christ our Lord
Affection sounds in ev'ry word;
" Thou art my chosen one he cries,
" Bound to my heart by various ties."

2 Sweet is thy voice, dear Lord, to me,
" I will behold no spot in thee;"

What

What mighty wonders love performs,
That puts a comeliness on worms!

3 Defil'd and lothesome as we are,
Thou mak'st us white, and call'st us fair
Adorn'st us with thy heav'nly dress,
Thy graces and thy righteousness.

4 O may my spirit daily rise,
On wings of faith above the skies;
Till death shall make my last remove,
To dwell for ever in thy love!

HYMN CXXXVIII. Long Metre. The Coll. A.

The sinner's Prayer.

When, gracious Lord, when shall it be
That I shall find my All in thee;
The fulness of thy promise prove,
The seal of thine eternal love?

2 Thee, only thee, I fain wou'd find,
And cast the world and flesh behind,
An helpless soul, I come to thee,
With only sin and misery.

3 Lord, I am sick, my sickness cure;
I want, do thou enrich the poor:
Under thy mighty hand I stoop,
O lift the abject sinner up.

4 LORD,

4 Lord, I am blind, be thou my sight;
  Lord, I am weak, be thou my might,
  An helper of the helpless be,
  And let me find my All in thee.

HYMN CXXXIX. Long Metre. The Coll. J.
Trust in God under Difficulties.

Why, O my heart, these anxious cares
  Why these tumultuous sick'ning fears?
Why thus all pensive and forlorn,
Dost thou thy thick'ning troubles mourn,

2 When threat'ning storms around thee rise
  And louring tempests spread the skies,
  On God, my soul, thy burden cast,
  And seek in him a peaceful rest.

3 If falshood and deceit abound,
  And envy's darts in secret wound,
  If earthly springs of comfort dry,
  And ev'ry blooming joy should die;

4 Silent I'll bear thy chast'ning rod,
  Thy just displeasure, O my God!
  On thee I'll wait with eager eyes,
  To thee my pray'r with hope shall rise.

5 Yes

AFTER SERMON.

5 Yes, I shall hear thy cheering voice;
In thee my soul shall yet rejoice;
Thou wilt reveal thy smiling face,
And hence these gloomy horrors chace,

6 Thou art my Saviour, thou my GOD!
Thy grace will I proclaim abroad;
That grace which bears my guilt away,
And turns the blackest night to day.

HYMN CXL. Long Metre. The Coll. *J.*
Christ the only Saviour.

1 LONG did my soul in JESUS' form,
   No comeliness nor beauty see;
His sacred name by others priz'd,
   Was tasteless still, and dead to me.

2 Men call'd me christian, and my heart
   On that delusion fondly stay'd;
Moral my hopes, my saviour self,
   Till mighty grace the cheat display'd.

3 Thanks to the hand that wak'd my dream
   That shew'd me wretched, naked, poor
That sweetly led me to the rock,
   Where all salvation stands secure.

4 Glad, I forsook my righteous pride,
    My moral, tarnish'd, sinful dress;
Exchang'd my dross away for Christ,
    And found the robe of righteousness.

CXLI. Long Metre. (Ps. cxlv.)   J.
The heart devoted to God.

1 My God, my King thy various praise
    Shall fill the remnant of my days,
Thy grace employ my humble tongue,
Till death and glory raise the song.

2 The wings of ev'ry hour shall bear,
Some thankful tribute to thine ear;
And ev'ry setting sun shall see,
New works of duty done for thee.

3 Let distant times and nations raise,
The long succession of thy praise:
And unborn ages make my song,
The joy and labor of their tongue.

4 But who can speak thy wond'rous deeds
Thy greatness all our thoughts exceeds,
Vast and unsearchable thy ways,
Vast and immortal be thy praise.

AFTER SERMON.

HYMN CXLII. Long Metre. Dr. Watts. J.
Gods promise unchangeable. Heb. vi. 17. 19.

HOW oft have sin and satan strove
   To rend my soul from thee my God
But everlasting is thy love,
   And Jesus seals it with his blood.

2 The oath and promise of the Lord,
   Join to confirm the wond'rous grace
Eternal pow'r performs the word,
   And fills all Heav'n with endless praise.

3 Amidst temptations sharp and long,
   My soul to this dear refuge flies;
Hope is my anchor, firm and strong,
   While tempests blow, and billows rise

4 The gospel bears my spirit up;
   A faithful and unchanging GOD,
Lays the foundation for my hope,
   In oaths, and promises, and blood.

HYMN CXLIII. Long Metre. Cannick. J.
The way to Canaan.

1 JESUS, my All, to heaven is gone,
   He, whom I fix my hope upon;
His track I see, and I'll pursue,
The narrow way, till him I view.

2 The

AFTER SERMON.

2 The way the holy prophets went,
   The road that leads from banishment;
   The King's high way of holiness,
   I'll go, for all his paths are peace.

3 This is the way I long have sought,
   And mourn'd because I found it not;
   My grief a burden long has been,
   Because I could not cease from sin.

4 The more I strove against its power,
   I sinn'd and stumbled yet the more;
   Till late I hear'd my Saviour say;
   " Come hither, soul, I am the way."

5 Lo! glad I come, and thou blest lamb,
   Shalt take me to thee as I am;
   Nothing but sin I thee can give,
   Nothing but love shall I receive.

6 Then will I tell poor sinners round,
   What a dear Saviour I have found;
   I'll point to thy redeeming blood;
   And say " Behold the way to God."

HYMN CXLIV. Long Metre. Lyric Poems. *J.*
The Law and Gospel.

1 CURST be the man for ever curst,
   " That doth one wilful sin commit;
   " Death

"Death and damnation for the first,
"Without relief and infinite."

2 Thus Sinai roars; and round the earth
Thunder, and fire, and vengeance flings;
But Jesus thy dear gasping breath,
And Calvary say gentler things.

3 "Pardon, and grace, and boundless love
"Streaming along a Saviour's blood,
"And life, and joys, and crowns above,
"Obtain'd by a dear bleeding God."

4 Hark how he prays, (the charming sound,
Dwell on his dying lips) forgive;
And every groan and gasping wound,
Cries, "Father, let the rebels live."

5 Go, you that rest upon the law,
And toil and seek salvation there,
Look to the flame that Moses saw,
And shrink, and tremble, and despair.

6 But I'll retire beneath the cross,
Saviour at thy dear feet I lie;
And the keen sword that justice draws,
Flaming and red, shall pass me by.

HYMN

HYMN CXLV. Long Metre. The Collection J.
Invitation.

1 SINNERS, obey the gospel word,
  Haste to the supper of your Lord;
  Be wise to know your gracious day;
  All things are ready, come away.

2 Ready the father is to own,
  And kiss his late returning son;
  Ready the loving Saviour stands,
  And spreads for you his bleeding hands.

3 Ready the spirit of his love,
  Just now the stony heart to move;
  T' apply, and witness with that blood,
  And wash, and seal you sons of God,

4 Ready for you the angels wait,
  To triumph in your blest estate:
  Tuning their harps, they long to praise,
  The wonders of redeeming grace.

5 Come then ye sinners, to your Lord,
  To happiness in Christ restor'd;
  His profer'd benefits embrace,
  And taste the fulness of his grace.

HYMN CXLVI. Long Metre. Dr. Watts. J.
The almost Christian.

1 BRoad is the road that leads to death,
    And thousands walk together there:
  But wisdom shews a narrow'r path,
  With here and there a traveller.

2 Deny thyself, and take thy cross,
  Is the Redeemer's great command!
  Nature must count her gold but dross,
  If she would gain this heavenly land.

3 The fearful soul, that tires and faints,
  And walks the ways of God no more;
  Is but esteemed almost a saint?
  And makes his own damnation sure.

4 Lord, let not all my hopes be vain,
  Create my heart entirely new;
  Which hypocrites could ne'er attain,
  Which false apostates never knew.

The same
CXLVII*. Long Metre. Dr. Watts. (Pf. 51.) J.
True Penitence.

1 SHEW pity Lord, O Lord forgive;
    Let a repenting rebel live.
  Are not thy mercies large and free?
  May not a sinner trust in thee?

AFTER SERMON.

2 My crimes are great, but not surpass;
The pow'r and glory of thy grace?
Great God, thy nature has no bound,
So let thy pard'ning love be found.

3 O wash my soul from ev'ry sin,
And make my guilty conscience clean,
Here on my heart the burden lies,
And past offences pain my eyes.

4 My lips with shame my sin confess,
Against thy law, against thy grace;
Lord should thy judgment grow severe,
I am condemn'd, but thou art clear.

5 Yet save a trembling sinner Lord,
Whose hope, still hovering round thy word
Wou'd light of some sweet promise there
Some sure support against despair

HYMN CXLVII. Long Metre. The Collection, *J.*
The stony Heart.

1 O! For a glance of heav'nly day,
To take this stubborn stone away;
And thaw with beams of love divine,
This heart, this frozen heart of mine.

2 The rocks can rent; the earth can quake,
The seas can roar; the mountains shake;

Of

Of feeling all things shew some sign,
But this unfeeling heart of mine.

3 To hear the sorrows thou hast felt,
Dear Lord an adamant would melt:
But I can read each moving line,
And nothing move this heart of mine.

4 Thy judgments too unmov'd I hear,
(Amazing thought!) which devils fear:
Goodness and wrath in vain combine,
To stir this stupid heart of mine.

5 But something yet can do the deed,
And that dear something much I need:
O! may thy Spirit now refine,
From dross, and melt this heart of mine.

HYMN CXLVIII. Long Metre. The Collection. *J.*

Satan repulsed.

1 'TIS false: thou vile accuser, go,
I see thro' all the thin disguise,
Back to thy native realms below,
Thou parent of deceit and lies!

2 Think not to drive my trembling soul,
Laden with guilt, to black despair;
Hast thou surveyed the sacred roll,
And found my name not written there.

AFTER SERMON.

3 Prefumptuous thought! to fix the bound
 To limit mercy's fovereign reign:
What other happy fouls have found,
 I'll feek, nor fhall I feek in vain.

4 I own my guilt thy charge confefs.
 Nor can thy malice make it more,
Of crimes already numberlefs,
 Vain the attempt to fwell the fcore.

5 Set the black lift before my fight;
 While I remember Jefus dy'd,
'Twill only urge my fpeedier flight,
 To feek falvation at his fide.

6 Low at his feet I'll caft me down,
 To him reveal my grief and fear;
And if he fpurns me from his throne,
 I'll be the firft who perifh there.

HYMN CXLIX. Long Metre. Dr. Watts.   *J*.
Remembering our Latter end.

1 NOW in the heat of youthful blood,
 Remember your Creator, God;
Behold the months come haft'ning on,
When you fhall fay my joys are gone.

2 Behold the aged finner goes,
 Laden with guilt and heavy woes,

Down

Down to the regions of the dead,
With endless curses on his head.

3 The dust returns to dust again;
The soul in agonies of pain,
Ascends to God; not there to dwell,
But hears her doom and sinks to hell.

4 Eternal King! I fear thy name;
Teach me to know how frail I am;
And when my soul must hence remove,
Give me a mansion in thy love.

HYMN CL. Long Metre. Dr. Watts. *J.*
The love of Christ shed abroad in the heart.

1 COME, dearest Lord, descend & dwell
By faith and love in ev'ry breast;
Then shall we know, and taste, and feel
The joys that cannot be express'd.

2 Come, fill our hearts with inward strength
Make our enlarged souls possess,
And learn the hight, and breadth, and length,
Of thine unmeasurable grace.

3 Now to the God whose pow'r can do,
More than our thoughts or wishes know,

Be

Be everlasting honours done
By all the church, thro' Christ his Son.

HYMN CLI. Long Metre.. Hart. J.

Dismiss us with thy blessing, Lord,
   Help us to feed upon thy word,
All that has been amiss, forgive,
And let thy truth within us live.

Tho' we are guilty, thou art good;
Wash all our works in JESUS' blood;
Give ev'ry fetter'd soul release,
And bid us all depart in peace.

CLII. Long Metre. (Pf. cxlv.) J.

ALL gracious God thy people bless
   Enrich their souls with ev'ry grace
May all receive thy precious word,
Ascribing glory to the LORD.

Let careless sinners now attend,
Before the means! and life shall end;
Excite attention to thy voice,
And bid the troubl'd soul rejoice,

Tho' from thy temple we depart,
Yet deign to dwell in ev'ry heart;
Keep us in all our ways, and be:
Our portion to eternity.-

HYMN

HYMN CLIII. Long Metre. The Coll. J.
The Mysteries of Providence.

1 LORD how mysterious are thy ways!
How blind are we, how mean our praise!
Thy steps can mortal eyes explore!
Tis ours to wonder and adore.

2 Thy deep decrees from creature sight
Are hid in shades of awful night;
Amid the lines, with curious eye,
Not angel-minds presume to pry.

3 Great God! I would not ask to see
What in futurity shall be;
If light and bliss attend my days,
Then let my future hours be praise.

4 Is darkness and distress my share?
Then let me trust thy guardian care
Enough for me, if love divine
At length thro' every cloud shall shine.

5 Yet this my soul desires to know,
Be this my only wish below;
That Christ is mine this great request
Grant, bounteous God: and I am blest.

HYMN

AFTER SERMON.

HYMN CLIV. Long Metre. The Coll. *J.*
A prayer.

BE with me, Lord, where 'ere I go;
Learn me what thou would'ft have me do;
Suggeft what'ere I think or fay;
Direct me in the narrow way.

2 Prevent me, left I harbour pride;
Left I in my own ftrength confide;
Shew me my weaknefs let me fee,
I have my pow'r my All from thee.

3 Enrich me always with thy love;
My kind protector ever prove;
Thy fignet put upon my breaft;
And let thy Spirit on me reft.

4 Afift, and teach me how to pray;
Incline my nature to obey,
What thou abhor'ft, that let me flee,
And only love what pleafes thee.

5 O may I never do my will,
But thine, and only thine fulfill;
Let all my time and all my ways,
Be fpent and ended in thy praife.

HYMN

HYMN CLV. Long Metre. The Coll. J.
To the Holy Ghost.

1 STAY, thou insulted Spirit, stay;
 Tho' I have done thee such despite,
Cast not a sinner quite away,
 Nor take thine everlasting flight.

2 Tho' I have most unfaithful been,
 Of all, who e'er thy grace receiv'd;
Ten thousand times thy goodness seen,
 Ten thousand times thy goodness griev'd.

3 But O! the chief of sinners spare,
 In honor of my great High Priest;
Nor in thy righteous anger swear
 T' exclude me from thy people's rest.

4 If yet thou canst my sins forgive,
 E'en now, O Lord, relieve my woes;
Into thy rest of love receive,
 And bless me with a calm repose.

5 E'en now my weary soul release
 And raise me by thy gracious hand;
Guide me into thy perfect peace,
 And bring me to the promis'd land.

AFTER SERMON.

HYMN CLVI. Long Metre. The Coll.   *J.*
Inconstancy.

1 LORD Jesus, when, when shall it be
   That I no more shall break with thee
When will this war of passion cease,
And my free soul enjoy thy peace?

2 Here I repent and sin again;
Now I revive, and now am slain;
Slain by the same unhappy dart,
Which O! too often wounds my heart!

3 O Saviour when, when shall I be,
A garden seal'd to all but thee?
No more expos'd, no more undone,
But live and grow to thee alone?

4 Guide thou, O Lord, guide thou my (course,
And draw me on with thy sweet force
Still make me walk, still make me tend;
By thee, my way, to God my end.

CLVII. Short Metre. (Ps. xxv.)   *J.*
Distress of Soul.

1 MINE eyes and my desire
   Are ever to the Lord.
I love to plead his promises,
And rest upon his word.

2 Turn, turn thee to my soul,
  Bring thy salvation near;
When will thy hand releaſe my feet
  Out of the deadly ſnare.

3 When ſhall the ſov'reign grace
  Of my forgiving God.
Reſtore me from thoſe dang'rous ways
  My wand'ring feet have trod!

4 The tumult of my thoughts
  Doth but increaſe my woe;
My ſpirit languiſhes, my heart,
  Is deſolate and low.

5 With every morning light
  My ſorrow now begins;
Look on my anguiſh and my pain,
  And pardon all my ſins.

HYMN CLVIII. Short Metre. Dr. Watts. *J.*
The paſſion and exaltation of Chriſt.

1 COME all harmonious tongues
    Your nobleſt muſick bring:
  'Tis Chriſt the everlaſting God,
    And Chriſt the man we ſing.

  Tell how he took our fleſh,
    To take away our guilt,

Sing

Sing the dear drops of sacred blood
  That hellish monsters spilt.

3 Down to the shades of death
    He bow'd his awful head;
  Yet he arose to life and reign
    When death itself is dead.

4 No more the bloody spear,
    The Cross and nails no more;
  For hell itself shakes at his name,
    And all the Heav'ns adore.

5 There the Redeemer sits,
    High on the Father's throne;
  The Father lays his vengeance by,
    And smiles upon his Son.

HYMN CLIX. Short Metre. The Coll.   J.
Christ justifies and sanctifies. (John xix. 24.)

1 MY Saviour's pierced side
    Pour'd out a double flood;
  By water we are purify'd,
    Ad pardon'd by thy blood.

2 Look up, my soul, to him,
    Whose death was thy desert;
  And humbly view the living stream
    Flow from his breaking heart.

E 2   3 There

3 There on the curſed tree
    In dying pangs he lies,
Fulfills his Father's great decree,
    And all our wants ſupplies.

4 Thus the Redeemer came,
    By water and by blood;
And when the Spirit ſpeaks the ſame,
    We feel his witneſs good.

5 LORD, cleanſe my ſoul from ſin;
    Nor let thy grace depart;
Great comforter, abide within,
    And witneſs to my heart.

HYMN CLX. Sort Metre. The Coll.   J.
Grace from. (Eph. ii. 5.)

1 GRACE! 'tis a charming ſound,
    Harmonious to the ear!
Heav'n with the echo ſhall reſound
    And all the earth ſhall hear.

2 Grace firſt contriv'd a way
    To ſave rebellious man;
And all the ſteps that grace diſplay,
    Which drew the wond'rous plan.

3 Grace taught my roving feet
    To tread the heav'nly road;

And

And new supplies each hour I meet,
  While pressing on to God.

4 Grace all the work shall crown,
   Thro' everlasting days;
  It lays in heav'n the topmost stone;
   And well deserves the praise.

HYMN CLXI. Short Metre. Dr. Doddridge. *J.*
Dismission.

1 NOW let our voices join.
   To form a sacred song;
  Ye Pilgrims in Jehovah's ways
   With musick pass along.

2 All honour to his name,
   Who marks the shining way;
  To him, who leads the wanderers on,
   To realms of endless day.

HYMN CLXII. Short Metre. Dr. Watts. *J.*
Faith in Christ our sacrifice.

1 NOT all the blood of beasts,
   On Jewish altars slain,
  Could give the guilty conscience peace,
   Or wash away one stain.

2 But Christ the heav'nly Lamb,
   Takes all our sins away;

A sacrifice of nobler name,
  And richer blood than they.

3 My faith would lay its hand,
  On that dear head of thine,
While like a penitent I stand,
  And there confess my sin.

4 My soul looks back to see,
  The burdens thou didst bear,
When hanging on the cursed tree,
  And hopes her guilt was there.

5 Believing we rejoice,
  To see the curse remove;
We bless the Lamb with cheerful voice,
  And sing his bleeding love.

HYMN CLXIII. Short Metre. The Coll. *J.*

1 AWAKE and sing the song,
  Of Moses and the Lamb;
Wake ev'ry heart and ev'ry tongue,
  To praise the Saviour's name.

2 Sing of his dying love,
  Sing of his rising pow'r,
Sing how he intercedes above,
  For those whose sins he bore.

3 Sing till we feel our hearts,
    Ascending with our tongues,
Sing 'till the love of sin departs,
    And grace inspires our songs.

4 Sing on your heav'nly way,
    Ye ransom'd sinners sing;
Sing on, rejoicing ev'ry day,
    In Christ the eternal King.

5 Soon shall ye hear him say,
    " Ye blessed children come;"
Soon will he call you hence away,
    And take his wand'rers home.

CLXIV. Short Metre. (Ps. xcix.)   J.
Christ's Kingdom and Majesty.

1 THE God Jehovah reigns,
    Let all the nations fear;
Let sinners tremble at his throne,
    And saints be humble there.

2 Jesus the Saviour reigns,
    Let earth adore its LORD;
Bright Cherubs his attendants stand,
    Swift to fulfill his word.

3 In Zion is his throne,
    His honours are divine;

AFTER SERMON.

His church shall make his wonders known
For there his glories shine.

4 How holy is his name!
How terrible his praise!
Justice and truth, and judgment join,
In all his works of grace.

HYMN CLXV. Short Metre. The Coll. *J.*

1 ONCE more before we part,
We'll bless the Saviour's name;
Record his mercies ev'ry heart,
Sing ev'ry tongue the same,

2 Hoard up his sacred word,
And feed thereon, and grow;
Go on to seek to know the LORD,
And practice what you know.

HYMN CLXVI. Short Metre. Dr. Watts. *J.*

Complaint of ingratitude.

1 IS this the kind return,
And these the thanks we owe?
Thus to abuse eternal love,
Whence all our blessings flow!

2 To what a stubborn frame,
Hath sin reduc'd our mind!

What

>   What strange rebellious wretches we,
>   And God as strangely kind!
>
> 3 Turn, turn us, mighty God!
>   And mould our souls afresh;
>   Break, sov'reign grace, these hearts of
>   And give us hearts of flesh   (stone,
>
> 4 Let old ingratitude,
>   Provoke our weeping eyes,
>   And hourly, as new mercies fall,
>   Let hourly thanks arise.

HYMN CLXVII. Short Metre.   *J.*

Dismission.

> 1 NOW, Lord, thy blessing add,
>   To what our ears have heard:
>   Pardon what thou hast seen amiss,
>   The truth let be rever'd.
>
> 2 May ev'ry soul improve,
>   Thy messages of grace,
>   Before our time shall cease to be,
>   And we shall end our race.
>
> 3 Keep us from ev'ry harm,
>   Especially from sin;
>   Direct us in the way of peace,
>   And safe to glory bring.

BAPTISM.

HYMN CLXVIII. Long Metre. Dr. Watts. *A.*

1 DO we not know that solemn word,
    That we are bury'd with the Lord;
Baptiz'd into his death and then,
Put off the body of our sin.

2 Our souls receive diviner breath,
    Rais'd from corruption, guilt and death;
So from the grave did Christ arise,
And lives to God above the skies.

3 No more let sin or satan reign,
    Over our mortal flesh again;
The various lusts we serv'd before,
Shall have dominion now no more.

HYMN CLXIX. Long Metre. Dr. Watts. *J.*
The Commission.

1 'TWas the commission of our Lord,
    Go, teach the nations and baptize,
The nations have receiv'd the word,
Since he ascended to the skies.

2 Repent and be baptiz'd he saith,
    For the remission of your sins,
And thus our sense assists our faith,
    And shews us what the Gospel means.

3 Our

3 Our souls he washes in his blood,
   As water makes the body clean;
Thus are our natures purify'd,
   From the defiling stains of sin.

4 Thus we engage ourselves to thee,
   And seal our cov'nant with the Lord;
O may the great eternal Three,
   In Heaven our solemn vows record.

HYMN CLXX. Common. Metre S. Stennett. A.

1 THus was the great Redeemer plung'd
      In Jordan's swelling flood;
   To shew, he'd one day be baptiz'd,
      In tears, in sweat and blood.

2 Thus was his sacred body laid,
   Beneath the yielding waves,
Thus was his sacred body rais'd
   Out of the liquid grave.

3 When lo! from realms of light and bliss,
   The heavenly dove comes down,
Lights on his venerable head,
   Which rays of glory crown.

4 While his eternal father's voice,
   An awful joy excites;

This is my well beloved son,
  In whom my soul delights.

5 Lord, thy own precept we obey,
  In thy own footsteps tread,
We die, are bury'd rise with thee
  From regions of the dead.

HYMN CLXXI. Long Metre. Newport. Coll. *A.*

1 THE great Redeemer we adore,
    Who came the lost to seek and save;
  Went humbly down from Jordan's shore
    To find a tomb beneath a wave.

2 Thus it becomes us to fulfil,
    All righteousness he meekly said,
  Why should we then to do his will,
    Or be ashamed or be afraid?

3 With thee into thy watr'y tomb,
    Lord 'tis our glory to descend;
  'Tis wondrous grace that gives us room,
    To lie interr'd with such a friend.

4 But a much more tempestuous flood,
    O'erwhelm'd thy body and thy soul:
  That's plung'd in tears and sweat & blood
    And over this black terrors roll.

5 Yet as the yielding waves give way,
      To let us see the light again:
   So on thy resurrection day,
   The bands of death prov'd weak & vain.

HYMN CLXXII. Long Metre. Alter'd by B. Francis.   J.

Baptism. Not asham'd of Christ.

1 JESUS! and shall it ever be?
      A mortal man ashamed of thee!
   Asham'd of thee, whom Angels praise
   Whose glories shine thro' endless days

2 Asham'd of Jesus! sooner far,
   Let ev'ning blush to own a star;
   He sheds the beams of light divine,
   O'er this benighted soul of mine.

3 Asham'd of Jesus! just as soon,
   Let midnight be asham'd of noon;
   'Tis midnight with my soul till He,
   Bright morning star bids darkness flee.

4 Asham'd of Jesus! that dear friend,
   On whom my hopes of Heav'n depend!
   No; when I blush, be this my shame,
   That I no more revere his name,

E 7   5 Asham'd

5 A sham'd of Jesus! yes I may,
  When I've no guilt to wash away;
  No tear to wipe, no good to crave,
  No fears to quell no soul to save.

6 Till then, nor is my boasting vain,
  Till then, I boast a Saviour slain!
  And O may this my glory be,
  That Christ is not asham'd of me.

HYMN CLXXIII. Long Metre. S. Stennett. J.

At Baptism.

1 SEE how the willing converts trace,
  The path their great Redeemer trod;
  And follow thro' his liquid grave,
  The meek, the lovely son of God!

2 Here they renounce their former deeds;
  And to a heav'nly life aspire,
  Their rags for glorious robes exchang'd
  They shine in clean and bright attire.

3 O sacred Rite! by thee the name,
  Of Jesus we to own begin:
  This is our resurrection pledge,
  Pledge of the pardon of our sin.

4 Glory to God on high be given,
  Who shews his grace to sinful men;

Let

BAPTISM.

Let Saints on earth and hosts in heav'n,
In concert join their loud amen.

HYMN CLXXIV. Long Metre. Trivett. A.

1 Now keep me stedfast dearest Lord,
 That I may serve thee with regard;
As one baptiz'd in thine own way,
And never let me from thee stray.

2 Lord give me strength for ev'ry day,
To do thy will, rejoice and pray;
Long have I liv'd and did not know
My strength must all from Jesus flow.

3 The work that he hath wrought for us
Doth testify it must be thus;
Come praise the Lord, 'tis he I know,
And of his mercy share below.

4 Come Lord, come quickly, come away,
Come quickly Lord, and with me stay;
Come Lord, and feed me with the sheep
And from henceforth forever keep,

5 Me where thy sweetest pastures be,
Till thou shall take me up to thee;
Till then when on my knees I cry,
Lord hear my prayer, send quick supply.

BAPTISM.

HYMN CLXXV. Short Metre. Newport Coll. *A.*

1 IN such a grave as this
       The meek Redeemer lay,
    When He our souls to seek and save
       Learn'd humbly to obey.

2 See how the spotless Lamb
       Descends into the stream!
    And teaches sinners not to scorn
       What him so well became.

3 His body sanctifies
       The salutary flood,
    And teaches us to plunge our souls
       In t'th' fountain of his blood.

4 Oh! Sinners wash away,
       Your sins of crimson dye,
    Bury'd with him your sins shall all,
       In dark oblivion lie.

5 Rise and ascend with him,
       A heavenly life to lead,
    Who came to rescue guilty men,
       From regions of the dead.

HYMN

HYMN CLXXVI. Common Metre. Dr. J. Stennett.

1 LORD, at thy Table I behold
   The wonders of thy grace;
But most of all admire that I
   Should find a welcome place.

2 (I that am all defil'd with sin,
   A rebel to my God.
I that have crucify'd his Son
   And trampled on his blood.)

3 What strange surprising grace is this,
   That such a soul has room!
My Saviour takes me by the hand,
   My Jesus bids me come.

4 Eat, O my friends the Saviour cries,
   The Feast was made for you;
For you I groan'd, and bled, and dy'd
   And rose, and triumph'd too.

5 With trembling faith, and bleeding
   Lord we accept thy love   (hearts,
'Tis a rich Banquet we have had,
   What will it be above.

6 Ye saints below, and Hosts of Heav'n,
   Join all your praising pow'rs:

No theme is like redeeming love,
  No Saviour is like ours.

7 Had I ten thousand hearts, dear Lord,
  I'd give them all to thee,
Had I ten thousand tongues, they all
  Should join the harmony.

HYMN CLXXVII. Common Metre. Dr. S. Stennett. J.
  My Flesh is Meat indeed. (John vi. 65.)

1 HERE at thy table, Lord, we meet,
  To feed on food divine;
Thy Body is the bread we eat,
  Thy precious blood the wine.

2 He that prepares this rich repast,
  Himself comes down and dies,
And then invites us thus to feast
  Upon the sacrifice.

3 Sure there was never love so free,
  Dear Saviour, so divine;
Well thou may'st claim that heart of me,
  Which owes so much to thine.

4 Yes, thou shalt surely have my heart,
  My soul, my strength, my all,
With life itself I'll freely part,
  My Jesus, at thy call.

HYMN

HYMN CLXXVIII. Common Metre. Dr. Watts. *J.*
Christ's dying love.

1 HOW condescending and how kind,
  Was God's eternal Son!
Our mis'ry reach'd his heav'nly mind,
  And pity brought him down.

2 This was compassion like a God,
  That when the Saviour knew,
The price of pardon was his blood,
  His pity ne'er withdrew.

3 Now tho' He reigns exalted high,
  His love is still as great:
Well He remembers calvary,
  Nor let his saints forget.

4 Here let our hearts begin to melt,
  While we his death record,
And, with our joy for pardon'd guilt,
  Mourn that we pierc'd the Lord.

HYMN CLXXIX. Common Metre. Dr. Watts. *J.*
Pardon and strength from Christ.

1 FATHER we wait to feel thy grace,
  To see thy glories shine;
The LORD will his own table bless,
  And make the feast divine.

       2 We

2 We touch, we taste the heav'nly bread,
 We drink the sacred cup;
With outward forms our sense is fed,
 Our souls rejoice in hope.

3 We shall appear before the throne
 Of our forgiving God,
Dress'd in the garments of his Son,
 And sprinkled with his blood.

4 We shall be strong to run the race,
 And climb the upper sky!
Christ will provide our souls with grace
 He bought a large supply.

HYMN CLXXX. Common Metre. Dr. Watts. *J.*
Divine Glories and Graces.

1 HOW are thy glories here displaid,
 Great God! how bright they shine,
While, at thy word, we break the bread,
 And pour the flowing wine!

2 Here thy revenging justice stands,
 And pleads its dreadful cause;
Here saving mercy spreads her hands
 Like Jesus on the cross.

3 Thy saints attend with ev'ry grace
 On this great sacrifice;
       And

And love appears with chearful face,
And faith with fixed eyes.

4 Our hope in waiting posture sits,
To heav'n directs her sight;
Here ev'ry warmer passion meets,
And warmer pow'rs unite.

5 Zeal and revenge perform their part,
And rising sin destroy;
Repentance comes with aching heart,
Yet not forbids the joy.

6 Dear Saviour, change our faith to sight,
Let sin forever die;
Then shall our souls be all delight,
And ev'ry tear be dry.

HYMN CLXXXI. Long Metre. Steele. *J.*
A dying Saviour.

1 STretch'd on the cross the Savior dies;
Hark! his expiring groans arise!
See, from his hands, his feet, his side,
Runs down the sacred crimson tide.

2 But life attends the deathful sound,
And flows from every bleeding wound;
The vital stream how free it flows,
To save and cleanse his rebel foes.

3 To suffer in the traytor's place.
　To die for man, surprising grace!
　Yet pass rebellious angels by;
　O why for man, dear Saviour why?

4 And didst thou bleed, for sinners bleed,
　And could the Sun behold the deed?
　No, he withdrew his sinking ray
　And darkness vail'd the mourning day.

5 Can I survey this scene of woe,
　Where ming'ling grief and wonder flow;
　And yet my heart unmov'd remain,
　Insensible to love or pain?

6 Come, dearest Lord, thy pow'r impart
　To warm this cold, this stupid heart;
　Till all its powers and passions move,
　In melting grief, and ardent love.

HYMN CLXXXII. Short Metre. Dr. Watts. *J.*

The Spirit, Water and blood. 1 John v. 6.

1 LET all our tongues be one,
　　To praise our GOD on high,
　Who from his bosom sent his Son,
　　To fetch us strangers nigh.

2 Nor let our voices cease,
　　To sing the Saviour's name;

Jesus

Jesus, th' ambassador of peace,
　　How chearfully he came!

3 It cost him cries and tears,
　　To bring us near to GOD;
Great was our debt and he appears,
　　To make the payment good.

4 Look up, my soul, to him,
　　Whose death was thy desert,
And humbly view the living stream,
　　Flow from his breaking heart.

5 There on the cursed tree,
　　In dying pangs he lies,
Fulfills his Father's great decree,
　　And all our wants supplies.

6 Thus the Redeemer came,
　　By water and by blood:
And when the Spirit speaks the same,
　　We feel his witness good.

HYMN CLXXXIII. Short Metre. The Coll. J.

1 COME, O my soul and sing,
　　How Jesus hath thee fed
How Jesus gave himself for thee,
　　The true and living bread

2 I love my Saviour Christ ;
 His grace did freely move,
And justly my affections claim ;
 I cannot help but love.

3 I love thee, O my LORD ;
 I gladly thee adore :
O may I never turn again !
 But love thee more and more.

4 O raise my feeble frame ;
 My little stock improve :
Increase my ardour day by day,
 And change me all to love.

HYMN CLXXXIV. Common Metre. The Coll. A.

1 THE LORD, how glorious is his face
 How kind his smiles appear !
And O ! what melting words he says,
 To ev'ry humble ear !

2 " For you, the children of my love,
 " It was for you I dy'd ;
 " Behold my bleeding hands and feet,
 " And look into my side."

3 These are the wounds for you I bore,
 The tokens of my pains,

When I came down to free your souls,
   From misery and chains.

4 When hell and all its spiteful pow'rs,
   Stood dreadful in the way;
To rescue those dear lives of yours,
   I gave my own away.

5 But while I bled, & groan'd, and dy'd,
   I ruin'd satan's throne;
High on the cross I hung and spy'd,
   The monster tumbling down.

6 Victorious GOD ! what can we pay,
   For favours so divine?
Here, LORD, we give our souls away,
   To be for ever thine.

HYMN. CLXXXV. Common Metre. (Pf. xxii.) *A*.

1 NOW from the roaring lion's rage,
   O LORD, protect thy Son,
Nor leave thy darling to engage,
   The pow'rs of hell alone.

2 Thus did our suffering Saviour pray,
   With mighty cries and tears;
God heard him in that dreadful day,
   And chas'd away his fears.

3 Great was the vict'ry of his death,
　　His throne exalted high;
　And all the kindreds of the earth,
　　Shall worship, or shall die.

4 A num'rous offspring must arise
　　From his expiring groans;
　They shall be reckon'd in his eyes,
　　For daughters and for sons.

5 The meek and humble souls shall see,
　　His table richly spread;
　And all that seek the Lord shall be,
　　With joys immortal fed.

Receiving a Member into the Church.

HYMN CLXXXVI. Common Metre. Trivett. *A.*
Receiving a member into the Church.

COME in ye bleſſed of our God,
   Come join the children here;
Waſh'd in our dying Saviour's blood,
   For Jeſus now appear.

Fellowſhip with us partake,
   Since room is found within,
By Chriſt prepar'd for ſick and weak,
   And cleanſing from their ſin.

Stay not within the wildernefs,
   Nor waiting at the door;
Come Jeſus will your wants redreſs,
   Were they ten thouſand more.

The ſick he leads, the filthy cleanſe,
   The guilty and diſtreſs'd,
He pardons, he forgives their ſins,
   And gives the weary reſt.

We've taſted of his grace, and know,
   His ordinances all;
As breaſts of conſolations flow,
   With peace for great and ſmall.

HYMN

LORD's SUPPER.

HYMN CLXXXVII. Commom Metre. Hart. A.

1 THAT doleful night before his death,
    The Lamb for sinners slain,
Did almost with his latest breath,
    This solemn feast ordain.

2 To keep thy feast, LORD, are we met;
    And to remember thee,
Help each poor trembler to repeat,
    For me, he died, *for me*.

3 Thy suff'rings, Lord, each sacred sign,
    To our rememb'rance brings:
We eat the bread and drink the wine;
    But think on nobler things.

4 O! tune our tongues, and set and frame,
    Each heart that pants to thee,
To sing, " Hosanna to the Lamb.
    " The Lamb that died for me."

HYMN CLXXXVIII. Common Metre. I. Stennett. J.

1 JESUS, O word divinely sweet!
    How charming is the sound!
What joyful news! what heavenly sense
    In that dear name is found!

2 Our souls all guilty, and condemn'd,
    In hopeless fetters lay;

Our

Our souls, with numerous sins deprav'd
  To death and hell a prey.

3 Jesus, to purge away this guilt,
  A willing victim fell,
And on his cross triumphant broke
  The bands of death and hell.

4 Our foes were mighty to destroy;
  He mighty was to save:
He dy'd, but could not long be held
  A prisoner to the grave.

5 Jesus, who mighty art to save,
  Still push thy conquests on;
Extend the triumphs of thy cross,
  Where'er the sun has shone.

6 O Captain of salvation! make
  Thy power and mercy known;
'Till crouds of willing converts come,
  And worship at thy throne.

HYMN CLXXXIX. Long Metre. Dr. Watts. *A.*

1 LORD, how divine thy comforts are!
  How heav'nly is the place,
Where Jesus spreads the sacred feast
  Of his redeeming grace!

2 There the rich bounties of our God,
 And fweeteft glories fhine;
There Jefus fays " that I am his,
 " And my beloved's mine."

3 " Here (fays the kind redeeming Lord,
 " And fhews his wounded fide)
 " See here the fpring of all your joys,
 " That open'd when I dy'd!"

4 He fmiles and chears my mournful heart
 And tells of all his pain.
 " All this (fays he) I bore for thee,"
 And then he fmiles again.

5 What fhall we pay our Heav'nly King.
 For grace fo vaft as this?
 He brings our pardon to our eyes
 And feals it with a kifs.

HYMN CXC. Metre. Dr. Watts. *A.*

1 COME let us join our chearful fongs
 With angels round the throne;
Ten thoufand, thoufand are their tongues
 But all their joys are one.

2 " Worthy the Lamb" that dy'd they cry,
 To be exalted thus;
 " Worthy

"Worthy the lamb," our lips reply,
   For he was slain for us.

3 Jesus is worthy to receive,
   Honour and pow'r divine;
And blessings more than we can give,
   Be Lord, for ever thine.

4 Let all that dwell above the sky.
   And air, and earth and seas;
Conspire to lift thy glories high,
   And speak thine endless praise.

5 Let all creation join in one,
   To bless the sacred name,
Of him that sits upon the throne,
   And to adore the Lamb.

HYMN CXCI. Long Metre. Dr. Watts.   *A.*

When I survey the wondrous cross,
   On which the Prince of glory dy'd,
My richest gain I count but loss,
   And pour contempt on all my pride

2 Forbid it Lord, that I should boast,
   Save in the cross of Christ my God;
All the vain things that charm me most
   I sacrifice them to his blood.

LORD's SUPPER.

3 See from his head, his hands, his feet,
   Sorrow and love flow mingl'd down!
Did e'er such love, such sorrow meet?
   Or thorns compose so rich a crown?

4 Were the whole realm of nature mine,
   That were a present far too small;
Love so amazing, so divine,
   Demands my soul, my life, my all.

HYMN CXCII. Long Metre. Dr. Watts. *A.*

1 JESUS! we bow before thy feet:
   Thy table is divinely stor'd;
Thy sacred flesh our souls have eat,
   'Tis living bread we thank the Lord.

2 And here we drink our Saviour's blood,
   We thank thee, Lord, 'tis gen'rous wine,
Mingled with love; the fountain flow'd
   From that dear bleeding heart of thine.

3 On earth is no such sweetness found,
   For thy dear flesh is heav'nly food;
In vain we search the world around,
   For bread so fine, or wine so good.

4 Carnal provisions can at best,
   But cheer the heart or warm the head,
                       But

But the rich cordial that we taste,
  Gives life eternal to the dead.

5 Joy to the master of the feast;
  His name our souls for ever bless;
 To God the King, and God the Priest,
  Aloud hosanna round the place.

HYMN CXCIII. Long Metre. Lyric Poems. *A.*
A bleeding Saviour.

What heavenly man, or lovely God,
  Comes marching downward from the
Array'd in garments roll'd in blood (skies
  With joy and pity in his eyes?

2 The Lord! the Saviour! yes, 'tis he,
  I know him by the smiles he wears;
Dear glorious man that dy'd for me,
  Drench'd deep in agonies and tears!

3 Lo, he reveals his shining breast;
  I own these wounds, and I adore:
Lo, he prepares a royal feast,
  Sweet fruit of the sharp pangs he bore

4 Whence flow these favours so divine!
  Lord! why so lavish of thy blood?
Why for such earthly souls as mine,
  This heav'nly flesh, this sacred food.

2 'Twas

5 'Twas his own love that made him bleed,
    That nail'd him to the curfed tree;
 'Twas his own love this table fpread,
    For fuch unworthy worms as we.

6 Then let us tafte the Saviour's love,
    Come faith, and feed upon the Lord;
 With glad confent our lips fhall move,
    And fweet hofannas crown'd the board.

CONSTITUTION OF A CHURCH

CXCIV. Common. Metre. (Pf. cxxxii.)   J.

1 ARISE, O King of grace, arife,
    And enter to thy reft,
 Lo! thy church waits with longing eyes
    Thus to be own'd and bleft.

2 Enter with all thy glorious train,
    Thy Spirit and thy word,
 All that the ark did once contain,
    Could no fuch grace afford,

3 Here mighty God, accept our vows,
    Here let thy praife be fpread;
 Blefs the provifion of thy houfe,
    And fill thy poor with bread.

4 Here

Here let the Son of David reign,
  Let God's anointed shine;
Justice and truth His court maintain,
  With love and power divine,

Here let him hold a lasting throne,
  And as his kingdom grows;
Fresh honours shall adorn his crown,
  And shame confound his foes.

HYMN CXCV. Lenox; &c. Dr. Doddridge. *J.*

GREAT Father of mankind,
  We bless that wondrous Grace,
Which could for Gentiles find,
  Within thy courts a place:
How kind the care our God displays,
  For us to raise a house of prayer.

Tho' once estranged far,
  We now approach the throne;
For JESUS brings us near,
  And makes our cause his own:
Strangers no more to thee we come,
  And find our home and rest secure.

To thee our souls we join,
  And love thy sacred name;

No more our own but thine,
    We triumph in thy claim;
Our Father King the covenant grace,
Our souls embrace thy titles sing.

4 May all the nations throng,
    To worship in thy house;
And thou attend the song,
    And smile upon their vows;
      Indulgent still,
      'Till earth conspire,
      To join the choir,
      On Zion's hill.

HYMN CXCVI. Proper Metre. 2 of 6 & of 8 &
    dit. (?? ??.) A.

1 HOW pleas'd and blest was I,
    To hear the people cry,
"Come let us seek our God to day!"
    Yes, with a cheerful zeal,
    We haste to Zion's hill,
And there our vows and honour pay.

2 Zion, thrice happy place,
    Adorn'd with wond'rous grace,
And walls of strength embrace thee round
    In thee our tribes appear,

                      To

To pray, and praife, and hear
The facred gofpel's joyful found.

3 There David's greater Son,
  Has fix'd his royal throne,
And fits for grace and judgement there;
  He bids the faints be glad
  He makes the finner fad,
And humble fouls rejoice with fear.

4 May peace attend thy gate,
  And joy within thee wait,
To blefs the foul of ev'ry gueft;
  The man that feeks thy peace,
  And wifhes thine increafe,
A thoufand bleffings on him reft!

HYMN CXCVII. Long Metre.   A.

1 LORD blefs thy faints affembled here
    In folemn cov'nant now to join,
  Unite them in thy holy fear,
    And in thy love their hearts combine

2 May they thy living members prove,
    Tho' all by nature once were dead;
  Be thou their Lord, their life, their love
    Their hufband, and their living head.

3 Thus constituted may they be,
  Part of thy gen'ral church below,
 Yet independant, but on thee,
  For thou alone their wants can know

4 O give this church a large increase,
  Of such as thou wilt own and bless;
 Lord fill their gates with joy and peace,
  And cloathe them with thy right'ousness

5 Make her a garden wall'd with grace,
  A temple built for God below;
 Where thy blest saints may see thy face;
  And fruits of thy bless'd spirit grow.

ORDINATION.

HYMN CXCVIII. Long Metre. Dr. Watts. *J.*
The effusion of the Spirit: or the success of the gospel.

1 GREAT was the day, the joy was great
  When the divine disciples met;
 While on their heads the Spirit came,
 And sat like tongues of cloven flame.

2 What gifts, what miracles he gave!
 And pow'r to give, and pow'r to save!

Furnish'd

Furnish'd their tongues, with wond'rous
  words,
Instead of shields, and spears, & swords.

3 Thus arm'd, he sent the champions forth
From east to west, from south to north:
" Go, and assert your Saviour's cause
" Go, spread the myst'ry of his cross.

4 These weapons of the holy war,
Of what Almighty force they are,
To make our stubborn passions bow,
And lay the proudest rebel low!

5 Nations, the learned and the rude,
Are by these heav'nly arms subdued,
While Satan rages at his loss,
And hates the doctrine of the cross.

HYMN CXCIX. Long Metre. Dr. Watts. J.
The Commission.

1 " GO preach my gospel, saith the
    " LORD,
  " Bid the whole earth my grace receive;
  " He shall be sav'd that trusts my word
  " He shall be damn'd that won't believe.

2 " Teach all the nations my commands,
  " I'm with you 'till the world shall end;
              " All

" All pow'r is trusted in my hands,
" I can destroy, and I defend.

3 He spake, and light shone round his head
On a bright cloud to heav'n he rode;
They to the farthest nations spread,
The grace of their ascended God.

HYMN CC. Common Metre. *A.*

1 THE presence of thy grace impart,
   And bless thy servants, Lord;
Thy glory may they have at heart:
   And guide them by thy word.

2 That whilst by prayer and solemn hands
   Thy servant they ordain;
They may respect thy bless'd commands,
   But hold traditions vain.

3 O may this servant set apart,
   Thy gospel to proclaim;
Ne'er from those sacred truths, depart
   Which glorify thy name.

4 If ordinances he attend;
   O make thy word his guide,
Nor suffer him e'er to depend,
   On any rule beside.

5 Then shall thy gospel, Lord, be crown'd,
   With a divine success:
Thy servant in thy grace abound;
   And thou his labours bless.

HYMN CCI. Common Metre. The Coll. *A.*

1 LET thy devoted servant go,
      Thy word, Lord, to proclaim;
   Thine only righteousness to show,
      And glorify thy name.

2 Grant him thine aid to speak thy word,
      With readiness each hour:
   Attend it with thy Spirit Lord,
      And let it come with power.

3 Open the hearts of all that hear,
      To make their Saviour room.
   O let them find redemption near,
      Let faith by hearing come.

4 Give them to hear the word as thine,
      Thy servant to receive;
   Lord prove thy truths with pow'r divine
      That sinners may believe.

* 5 Then shall thy servant joyful preach,
      Thy grace so wide, so free,

The verses marked with * are added being entirely new.

Nor ever cease the ways to teach,
That lead, O LORD, to thee.

HYMN CCII. Long Metre. The Coll.   *A.*

1 WITH all thy pow'r, O Lord defend
Him whom we now to thee commend;
A faithful minister secure,
And make him to the end endure.

2 Gird him with all sufficient grace;
Give to his footsteps paths of peace;
Thy truth and faithfulness fulfil;
Preserve him, Lord, from ev'ry ill.

3 Before his face protection send;
O love him, save him to the end:
Nor let him as thy pilgrim rove,
Without the convoy of thy love.

4 Enlarge, enflame, and fill his heart,
In him thy mighty power exert;
That thousands yet unborn may praise
The wonders of Redeeming grace.

HYMN CCIII. Short Metre. Dr. Watts.   *A.*

1 HOW beauteous are their feet,
Who stand on Zion's hill!

Who bring salvation on their tongues,
  And word's of peace reveal.

2 How charming is their voice!
  How sweet the tidings are!
" Zion, behold thy Saviour King,
" He reigns and triumphs here."

3 How happy are our ears,
  That hear this joyful sound,
Which kings and prophets waited for,
  And sought but never found!

4. How blessed are our eyes.
  That see this heav'nly light;
Prophets and kings desir'd it long,
  But dy'd without the sight!

5 The watchmen join their voice,
  And tuneful notes employ;
Jerusalem breaks forth in songs,
  And deserts learn the joy.

At an ASSOCIATION.

HYMN CCIV. Long Metre. Beddome. *J.*
A prayer for Ministers.

1 FATHER of mercies, bow thine ear
  Attentive to our earnest prayer;

We plead for thofe who plead for thee,
Succefsful pleaders may they be! (charge

2 How great their work, how vaft their
  Do thou their anxious fouls enlarge,
  Their beft acquirements are our gain,
  We fhare the bleffings they obtain.

3 Clothe them with Energy divine,
  Their words, and let thofe words be thine
  To them thy facred truth reveal,
  Supprefs their fear, inflame their zeal.

4 Teach them to fow the precious feed,
  Teach them thy chofen flock to feed:
  Teach them immortal fouls to gain,
  Souls which will well reward their pain.

5 Let thronging multitudes around,
  Hear from their lips the joyful found;
  In humble ftrains thy grace implore,
  And feel thy new creating power.

6 Let finners break their maffy chains,
  Diftreffed fouls forget their pains;
  Let light thro' diftant realms be fpread.
  And Zion rear her drooping head.

HYMN

HYMN CCV. Long Metre. Francis. J.
Ministers abounding in the work of the Lord.

1 BEFORE thy throne, eternal King,
Thy ministers their tribute bring,
Their tribute of united praise,
For heav'nly news and peaceful days.

2 We sing the conquests of thy sword,
And publish loud thy healing word:
While angels sound thy glorious name,
Thy saving grace our lips proclaim.

3 Thy various service we esteem,
Our sweet employ, our bliss supreme;
And, while we feel thy heav'nly love,
We burn like seraphim above.

4 Nor seraphs there can ever raise,
With us, an equal song of praise:
They are the noblest work of GOD,
But we the purchase of his blood.

5 Still in thy work would we abound;
Still prune the vine, or plow the ground,
Thy sheep with wholesom pasture feed,
And watch them with unwearied heed.

6 Thou art our LORD, our life, our love
Our care below, and crown above:

Thy praiſe ſhall be our beſt employ,
Thy preſence our eternal Joy.

HYMN CCVI. Common Metre. Newport Coll. *A.*
At meeting.

WELL met, dear friends in Jeſus' name
   Come let us now rejoice,
While we our Saviour's praiſe proclaim
   With cheerful heart and voice.

But, O dear Jeſus, Lamb of GOD,
   Send down the heav'nly dove,
His graces to diffuſe abroad,
   And warm our hearts with love!

In vain, dear Saviour, here we meet,
   Except thy face we ſee:
Thy preſence makes a heav'n moſt ſweet
   Where e'er we meet with thee.

Then O dear Jeſus condeſcend,
   To meet us with a ſmile,
Thy Spirit's quick'ning infl'ence ſend,
   And purge our hearts from guile,

That at the cloſe each one may ſay,
   We met not here in vain,

For we have tasted heaven to day,
Nor could we more contain.

HYMN CCVII. Long Metre.   *A.*

1 ENCOURAG'D by thy holy word,
   Thy churches thus conven'd, O Lord
By us, their dele gates elect,
Crave thy blest Spirit to direct.

2 O guide us by thy grace, to know,
What best promotes thy cause below;
And may our consultations be,
Fresh means to lead us, *Lord to thee.*

3 Lord let the glory of thy name,
And Zion's int'rest be our aim;
From ev'ry selfish motive free,
Devoted wholy, *Lord to thee.*

4 Associated year by year,
From all thy churches may we hear,
Of souls that to thy altars flee,
Dependant wholy *Lord on thee.*

5 The labours of thy servants bless,
In turning souls to righteousness;
That many converts they may see:
Yet give the glory *Lord to thee.*

FASTS AND THANKSGIVING.

HYMN CCVIII. Common Metre, (Pf. xviii.) *J.*

Thanksgiving for victory.

1 TO thine Almighty arm we owe,
    The triumphs of the day;
  Thy terrors Lord, confound the foe,
  And melt their strength away.

2 'Tis by thine aid our troops prevail,
    And break united pow'rs,
  Or burn their boasted fleets, or scale
  The proudest of their tow'rs.

3 How have we chas'd them thro' the field,
    And trod them to the ground,
  While thy salvation was our shield,
  But they no shelter found.

4 In vain to idol Saints they cry,
    And perish in their blood;
  Where is a rock so great so high,
  So pow'rful as our God.

5 The rock of Israel ever lives,
    His name be ever blest;
  'Tis his own arm the vict'ry gives,
  And gives his people rest.

HYMN

FASTS AND THANKSGIVING.

HYMN CCIX. Long Metre. Prefident Davies. *J.*
National Judgments deprecated, and national Mercies pleaded
Amos. 3. 1. 6.

1 While o'er our guilty land, O Lord!
    We view the terrors of thy fword
Oh! whither fhall the helplefs fly?
To whom but thee direct their cry?

2 The helplefs finner's cries and tears,
Are grown familiar to thine ears;
Oft has thy mercy fent relief,
When all was fear and hopelefs grief.

3 On thee our guardian God, we call,
Before thy throne of grace we fall;
And is there no deliv'rance there?
And muft we perifh in defpair?

4 See, we repent, we weep, we mourn,
To our forfaken God we turn;
O fpare our guilty country, fpare, (here
The church which thou has planted

5 We plead thy grace indulgent God;
We plead thy Son's atoning blood;
We plead thy gracious promifes,
And are they unavailing pleas?

F 7   6 Thefe

6 These pleas, presented at thy throne,
Have brought ten thousand blessings down
On guilty lands in helpless woe;
Let them prevail to save us too.

HYMN CCX. Long Metre. Steel. *J.*
On a day of prayer for success in war.

LOrd, how shall wretched sinners dare
Look up to thy divine abode:
Or offer their imperfect prayer,
Before a just a holy God.

2 Bright terrors guard thy awful seat,
And dazzling glories veil thy face:
Yet mercy calls us to thy feet,
Thy throne is still a throne of grace.

3 O may our souls thy grace adore,
May Jesus plead our humble claim;
While thy protection we implore,
In his prevailing glorious name.

4 Let past experience of thy care,
Support our hope, our trust invite;
Again attend our humble prayer,
Again be mercy thy delight.

5 Our arms succeed our councils guide,
Let thy righthand our cause maintain

FASTS and THANKSGIVING.

Till war's destructive rage subside,
 And peace resume her gentle reign.

HYMN CCXI. Long Metre. Rippon's Coll. *J.*
 Thanksgiving for national deliverance.

PRaise to the Lord, who bows his ear
 Propitious to his people's prayer,
And, tho' deliverance long delay,
Answers in his well chosen day.

Salvation doth to God belong;
His power and grace shall be our song,
The tribute of our love we bring,
To thee our Saviour, and our King!

Our temples guarded from the flame,
Shall echo thy triumphant name;
And every peaceful private home;
To thee a temple shall become.

Still be it our supreme delight,
To walk as in thy honor'd sight;
Hence in thy precepts and thy fear,
'Till life's last hour to persevere.

HYMN CCXII. Long Metre. Steel. *J.*
 Praise for national Peace.

GREAT ruler of the earth and skies,
 A word of thy Almighty breath

Can sink the world, or bid it rise:
Thy smile is life, thy frown is death.

2 When angry nations rush to arms,
And rage, and noise, and tumult reign
And war resounds its dire alarms,
And slaughter spreads the hostile plains

3 Thy sovereign eye looks calmly down,
And marks their course, and bounds their pow'r;
Thy word the angry nations own,
And noise and war are heard no more.

4 Then peace returns with balmy wing,
(Sweet peace! with her what blessings fled!)
Glad plenty laughs, the vallies sing,
Reviving Commerce lifts her head.

5 Thou good, and wise, and gracious Lord
All move subservient to thy will;
And peace and war await thy word,
And thy sublime Decrees fulfil.

6 To thee we pay our grateful songs,
Thy kind protection still implore;
O may our hearts, and lives, and tongues
Confess thy goodness and adore.

HYMN

FASTS AND THANKSGIVING.

HYMN CCXIII. Common Metre. Rippon's Coll. J.
Thanksgiving for victory.

1 TO thee who reign'ſt ſupreme above,
　　And reign'ſt ſupreme below,
Thou God of wiſdom, power, and love
　　We our ſucceſſes owe.

2 The thundering horſe, the martial band
　　Without thine aid were vain;
And victory flies at thy command,
　　To crown the bright campaign.

3 Thy mighty arm, unſeen, was nigh,
　　When we our foes aſſail'd;
'Tis thou haſt rais'd our honours high,
　　And o'er their hoſts prevail'd.

4 To our young race will we proclaim,
　　The mercies GOD has ſhown;
That they may learn to bleſs thy name
　　And chooſe him for their own.

5 Thus, while we ſleep in ſilent duſt,
　　When threat'ning dangers come,
Their Father's GOD ſhall be their truſt,
　　Their Refuge and their home.

HYMN

FOR A PUBLIC FAST.

HYMN CCXIV. Common Metre. Rippon's Coll. A.

1 WHEN Abra'm, full of sacred awe
  Before Jehovah stood,
And, with a humble fervent prayer,
  For guilty Sodom sued;

2 With what success, what wondrous grace
  Was his petition crown'd!
The LORD would spare, if in the place
  Ten righteous men were found.

3 And could a single, holy Soul,
  So rich a boon obtain?
Great God, and shall a nation cry,
  And plead with thee in vain?

4 Are not the righteous dear to thee,
  Now as in ancient times?
Or does this sinful land exceed,
  Gomorrah in its crimes?

5 Still are we thine, we bear thy name,
  Here yet is thine abode;
Long has thy presence bless'd our land,
  Forsake us not, O GOD.

HYMN CCXV. Common Metre. Rippon's Coll. A.

1 SEE, gracious God, before thy throne
  Thy mourning people bend

'Tis

For a Public Fast.

'Tis on thy sovereign grace alone,
  Our humble hopes depend.

Tremendous judgements from thy hand
  Thy dreadful power display;
Yet mercy spares this guilty land,
  And still we live to pray.

Why is America thus spar'd,
  Ungrateful as we are!
O make thy awful warnings heard,
  While mercy cries, "Forbear."

Sinners regardless of thy frown,
  Their pleasures they require;
And sink with gay indifference down,
  To everlasting fire.

O turn us, turn us, mighty Lord,
  By thy resistless grace;
Then shall our hearts obey thy word,
  And humbly seek thy face.

HYMN CCXVI. Common Metre. Hart. A.

LORD, look on all assembled here;
  Who in thy presence stand,
To offer up united pray'r,
  For this our sinful land.

2 Oft have we, each in private pray'd,
　　Our country might find grace,
　Now hear the same petitions made,
　　In this appointed place.

3 Or, if amongst us some be met,
　　So careless of their sin,
　They have not cried for mercy yet,
　　Lord, let them now begin.

4 Thou, by whose death poor sinners live
　　By whom their pray'rs succeed,
　Thy spir't of supplication give,
　　And we shall pray indeed.

5 Whatever be our destin'd case,
　　Accept us in thy Son;
　Give us his gospel, and his grace:
　　And then thy will be done.

HYMN CCXVII. Common Metre. The Coll. A.

1 THE Lord my shepherd and my guide
　　Will all my wants supply;
　In safety I shall still abide,
　　Beneath his watchful eye.

2 Tho' hast'ning to the silent tomb,
　　And death's dark shades appear;
　Thy presence, Lord, shall cheer the gloom
　　And banish ev'ry fear.

3 No

3 No evil can my soul dismay,
    While I am near my GOD;
My comfort, my support, and stay,
    Thy staff and guiding rod.

4 Thy constant bounties me surround,
    Amidst my envious foes;
My favour'd head with gladness crown'd,
    My cup with blessings flows.

5 Thus shall thy goodness love and care,
    Attend my future days;
And I shall dwell for ever near,
    My God, and sing his praise.

HYMN CCXVIII. Common Metre. Addison. 4.

1 WHEN all thy mercies, O my God
    My rising soul surveys,
Transported with the view I'm lost,
    In wonder, love, and praise.

2 Thy providence my life sustain'd
    And all my wants redrest,
When in the silent womb I lay,
    And hung upon the breast.

3 Unnumber'd comforts to my soul
    Thy tender care bestow'd,

Before my infant heart conceiv'd
From whom those comforts flow'd.

4 When in the slipp'ry paths of youth,
With heedless steps I ran;
Thine arm, unseen, convey'd me safe,
And led me on to man.

5 When worn by sickness oft hast thou
With health renew'd my face;
And when in sins and sorrows sunk,
Reviv'd my soul with grace.

6 Thy bounteous hand with worldly bliss
Has made my cup run o'er;
And in a kind and faithful friend
Has doubl'd all my store.

7 Thro' ev'ry period of my life,
Thy goodness I'll pursue;
And after death in distant worlds,
The glorious theme renew.

8 When nature fails, and day, and night
Divide thy works no more;
My ever grateful heart O Lord,
Thy mercy shall adore.

9 Thro' all eternity to thee,
A joyful song I'll raise

For O eternity's too short
  To utter all thy praise.

FASTS AND THANKSGIVING.

HYMN CCXIX. Common Metre. Rippon's Coll. J. *Harvest.*

1 TO praise the ever bounteous Lord
    My soul, wake all thy powers:
  He calls, and at his voice come forth,
    The smiling harvest hours.

2 His cov'nant with the earth he keeps;
    My tongue his goodness sing:
  Summer and winter know their time,
    His harvest crowns the spring.

3 Well pleas'd the toiling swains behold,
    The waving yellow crop:
  With joy they bear the sheaves away,
    And sow again in hope.

4 Thus teach me, gracious GOD, to sow
    The seeds of righteousness:
  Smile on my soul, and with thy beams
    The ripening harvest bless.

5 Then, in the last great harvest, I,
    Shall reap a glorious crop:
  The harvest shall by far exceed,
    What I have sown in hope.

HYMN

At a FUNERAL.

HYMN CCXX. Common Metre. Steel. J.

WHEN blooming youth is snatch'd
 By death's resistless hand (away,
Our hearts the mournful tribute pay,
 Which pity must demand.

2 While pity prompts the rising sigh,
 O may this truth, impress,
With awful power, I too must die,
 Sink deep in every breast.

3 Let this vain world engage no more;
 Behold the gaping tomb!
It bids us seize the present hour,
 To morrow death may come.

4 The voice of this alarming scene,
 May every heart obey;
Nor be the heav'nly warning vain,
 Which calls to watch and pray.

5 O let us fly, to Jesus fly,
 Whose powerful arm can save;
Then shall our hopes ascend on high,
 And triumph o'er the grave.

6 Great GOD, thy sovereign grace impart
 With cleansing, healing power;

This only can prepare the heart,
 For death's surprising hour.

HYMN CCXXI. Common Metre. Dr. Watts. J.
Life and Eternity.

THEE we adore, eternal name!
 And humbly own to thee,
How feeble is our mortal frame,
 What dying worms we be!

Our wasting lives grow shorter still,
 As months and days increase;
And ev'ry beating pulse we tell,
 Leaves one the number less.

The year rolls round, and steals away
 The breath that first it gave;
What e'er we do, where e'er we be,
 We're trav'lling to the grave.

Dangers stand thick thro' all the ground
 To push us to the tomb;
And fierce diseases wait around,
 To hurry mortals home.

Great GOD! on what a slender thread
 Hang everlasting things;
Th' eternal states of all the dead,
 Upon life's feeble strings.

6 Infinite

6 Infinite joy or endless woe,
    Attend on ev'ry breath;
And yet how unconcern'd we go,
    Upon the brink of death.

7 Waken, O LORD, our drowsy sense,
    To walk this dang'rous road;
And if our souls are hurry'd hence,
    May they be found with God.

HYMN CCXXII. Common Metre. Hughes' Coll. J.
Death's a Warning.

1 VAIN man thy fond pursuits forbear
    Repent thy end is nigh,
Death at the farthest can't be far;
    Oh think before you die!

2 Reflect thou hast a soul to save;
    Thy sins how high they mount!
What are thy hopes beyond the grave?
    How stands that dark account!

3 Death enters and there's no defence,
    His time there's none can tell,
He'll in a moment calls thee hence,
    To Heaven or to hell.

4 Thy flesh perhaps thy chiefest care,
    Shall crawling worms consume,

But ah! destruction stops not there;
  Sin kills beyond the tomb!

To day, the gospel calls, to day;
  Sinners, it speaks to you;
Let every one forsake his way,
  And mercy will ensue.

Rich mercy, dearly bought with blood,
  How vile soe'er he be;
Abundant pardon, peace with GOD;
  All giv'n entirely free.

HYMN CCXXIII. Long Metre. Fawcett.   J.
The death of the Sinner and the Saint.

WHAT scenes of horror & of dread,
  Await the sinner's dying bed!
Death's terrors all appear in sight,
Presages of eternal night.

His sins in dreadful order rise,
And fill his soul with sad surprise;
Mount Sinai's thunder stuns his ears,
And not one ray of hope appears.

Tormenting pangs distract the breast,
Where'er he turns, he finds no rest;
Death strikes the blow, he groans & cries
And, in despair and horror, dies.

4 Not so the heir of heavenly bliss;
His soul is fill'd with conscious peace;
A steady faith subdues his fear;
He sees the happy Canaan near.

5 His mind is tranquil and serene,
No terrors in his looks are seen;
His Saviour's smile dispels the gloom,
And smooths his passage to the tomb.

6 Lord, make my faith and love serene,
My judgement sound, my conscience clean
And when the toils of life are past,
May I be found in peace at last.

HYMN CCXXIV. Common Metre. Dr. Watts. J.

Death and Glory.

1 MY soul, come meditate the day
And think how near it stands,
When thou must quit this house of clay
And fly to unknown lands.

2 And you, mine eyes, look down & view
The hollow gaping tomb;
This gloomy prison waits for you,
Whene'er the summons come.

3 O! could we die with those that die,
And place us in their stead,

Then

> Then would our spirits learn to fly,
> And converse with the dead.

4 Then should we see the saints above,
> In their own glorious forms,
> And wonder why our souls should love
> To dwell with mortal worms.

5 How should we scorn these cloths of flesh,
> These fetters, and this load;
> And long for ev'ning to undress,
> That we may rest with GOD.

6 We should almost forsake our clay,
> Before the summons come,
> And pray, and wish our souls away,
> To their eternal home.

HYMN CCXXV. Common Metre. Dr. Watts. J.

A Funeral Thought.

HARK! from the tombs a doleful sound
> My ears attend the cry;
> " Ye living men, come view the ground
> " Where you must shortly lie.

2 " Princes, this clay must be your bed,
> " In spite of all your tow'rs;
> " The tall, the wise, the rev'rend head
> " Must lie as low as ours.

3 Great God! is this our certain doom!
   And are we still secure!
 Still walking downward to our tomb,
   And yet prepare no more!

4 Grant us the pow'rs of quick'ning grace
   To fit our souls to fly;
 Then, when we drop this dying flesh,
   We'll rise above the sky.

HYMN CCXXVI. Long Metre. Dr. Watts. *A.*

WHY should we start or fear to die,
   What tim'rous worms we mortals
 Death is the gate of endless joy, (are,
   And yet we dread to enter there.

2 The pains, the groans, and dying strife,
   Fright our approaching souls away;
 Still we shrink back again to life,
   Fond of our prison and our clay.

3 O! If my Lord would come and meet,
   My soul should stretch her wings in haste
 Fly fearless thro' death's iron gate,
   Nor feel the terrors as she pass'd.

4 Jesus can make a dying bed,
   Feel soft as downy pillows are,

While

While on his breast I lean my head,
  And breathe my life out sweetly there.

CCXXVII. Long Metre. (Ps. lxxxix.) A.

Remember, Lord our mortal state,
How frail our life, how short the date
Where is the man that draws his breath,
Safe from disease, secure from death?

2 Lord, while we see whole nations die,
Our flesh and sense repine and cry,
" Must death forever rage and reign!
" Or hast thou made mankind in vain."

3 Where is thy promise to the just?
Are not thy servants turn'd to dust?
But faith forbids these mournful sighs,
And sees the sleeping dust arise.

4 That glorious hour, that dreadful day
Wipes the reproach of saints away,
And clears the honour of thy word:
Awake our souls and bless the Lord.

HYMN CCXXVIII. Short Metre. Dr. Watts. A.

1 AND must this body die,
  This mortal frame decay?
And must these active limbs of mine,
  Lie mould'ring in the clay?

2 Corruption,

2 Corruption, earth, and worms,
　　Shall but refine this flesh,
　Till my triumphant spirit comes,
　　To put it on afresh.

3 God my Redeemer lives,
　　And often from the skies,
　Looks down and watches all my dust,
　　Till he shall bid it rise.

4 Array'd in glorious grace,
　　Shall these vile bodies shine,
　And ev'ry shape and ev'ry face,
　　Look heav'nly and divine.

5 These lively hopes we owe,
　　To Jesus' dying love,
　We would adore his grace below,
　　And sing his pow'r above.

CCXXIX. Short Metre. (Ps. xc.) A.

1 LORD what a feeble piece,
　　Is this our mortal frame?
　Our life how poor a trifle t'is,
　　That scarce deserves the name.

2 Alas the brittle clay,
　　That built our body first!

And

And ev'ry month and ev'ry day,
  'Tis mould'ring back to dust.

3 Our moments fly apace,
    Nor will our minutes stay;
  Just like a flood our hasty days,
    Are sweeping us away.

4 Well if our days must fly,
    We'll keep their end in sight;
  We'll spend them all in wisdom's way,
    And let them speed their flight.

5 They'll waft us sooner o'er,
    This life's tempestuous sea:
  Soon we shall reach the peaceful shore,
    Of blest eternity.

HYMN CCXXX. Common Metre. Dr. Watts *A*.

WHY do we mourn departed friends
    Or shake at death's alarm?
  'Tis but the voice that Jesus sends,
    To call them to his arms.

2 Why should we tremble to convey
    Their bodies to the tomb?
  There the dear flesh of Jesus lay,
    And left a long perfume:

3 The

3 The graves of all the saints he bless'd,
    And soft'ned ev'ry bed:
Where should the living members rest,
    But with the dying head.

4 Thence he arose, and burst the chain,
    To shew our feet the way,
From shades where death & darkness reign
    To realms of endless day.

5 Then let the last loud trumpet sound,
    And bid his kindred rise;
Awake, ye nations under ground;
    Ye saints, ascend the skies.

HYMN CCXXXI. Common Metre. Rippon's Coll. *A*.

Why should our mourning thoughts de-
    To grovel in the dust?   (light,
Or why should streams of tears unite,
    Around th' expiring just?

2 Did not the Lord our Saviour die,
    And triumph o'er the grave?
Did not our Lord ascend on high,
    And prove his power to save?

3 Doth not the sacred Spirit come,
    And dwell in all the saints?

And

And should the temples of his grace,
　　　　Resound with long complaints?

4　Awake, my soul, and like the sun,
　　　　Burst thro' each sable cloud;
　　And thou, my voice, tho' broke with
　　　　Tune forth thy songs aloud.　(sighs,

5　The spirit rais'd my Saviour up,
　　　　When he had bled for me;
　　And spite of death and hell shall raise
　　　　Thy pious friends and thee.

HYMN CCXXXII. Common Metre. Trivetts. A.

MY God! my God! and must I die,
　　　　Thy presence to behold;
　　Lord break the bands, and let me fly,
　　　　To tread the streets of gold.

2　Learn me to dwell on things above,
　　　　And sing as saints do there;
　　Those brightest objects of thy love,
　　　　And quickly me prepare.

3　To drop the body, and remove,
　　　　To yonder worlds on high;
　　Fain on thy wings celestial dove,
　　　　My soul would thither fly,

4 Yet trembling at each swelling wave,
　Of death's cold flood I stand;
Afraid to launch in them and leave,,
　This body and this land.

5 But if my Jesus I could hear,
　And see him standing by;
My soul would mount beyond her fear,
　Thro' death for Heaven fly.

HYMN CCXXXIII. Long Metre. Trivetts. *A.*
Funeral occasions.

1 DEATH as a sleep or gentle dose,
　Does every weary saint compose
Lays all its pain, and griefs remove,
Conveys the Soul to worlds above.

2 Where all its sighs and mournful cries,
With pained heart; and flowing eyes,
Are chang'd for pleasures lasting sweet
Nor can it more with sorrow meet.

3 Blest in the lamb's embrace it lies,
Praising its God above the skies;
In sparkling robes of glory bright,
Transporting joys and pure delight.

4 Thus with the growing concert join,
And seraphs in musick divine

'Tis

'Tis rapture almost ravishing,
To hear the charming notes they sing,

5 Nor can those joys sublime be less,
They're flowing streams of perfect bliss
Yet parents and relations dear,
Are loth their loving friend to spare.

HYMN CCXXXIV. Long Metre. Trivett. A.

WE needs must die, who banish'd lie
  Cloth'd with corrupt mortality;
And drop these cloaths of sinful clay,
Within the silent grave to lay.

2 God no man's person so respects;
He fairest jewels, though select,
To dwell with Christ in majesty,
Must need submit, wither, and die.

3 'Tis not in mortal bodies we,
Jehovah's face can ever see;
But are as water on the ground,
'Till Christ the jub'lee trumpet sound.

4 Then he that did our ransom pay,
Will clothe the saints in bright array,
As from the beds of dust they rise,
More splendid than the sparkling skies.

5 Wrapt

5 Wrapt in immortal beauties bright,
   Transcendant pleasures and delight;
   And while each saint his friend embrace
   The growing raptures will increase.

HYMN CCXXXV. Common Metre. Dr. Watts. *J.*

Evening.

DREAD sov'reign let my ev'ning song
    Like holy incense rise;
Assist the off'rings of my tongue
    To reach the lofty skies.

2 Thro' all the dangers of the day
    Thy hand was still my guard,
And still to drive my wants away,
    Thy mercy stood prepar'd.

Perpetual blessings from above
    Encompass me around,
But O how few returns of love,
    Hath my creator found?

4 What have I done for him that dy'd
    To save my wretched soul?
How are my follies multiply'd,
    Fast as my minutes roll!

5 Lord, with this guilty heart of mine,
    To thy dear cross I flee,

And

And to thy grace my soul resign,
  To be renew'd by thee.

6 Sprinkled afresh with pard'ning blood,
  I lay me down to rest,
As in th' embraces of my God,
  Or on my Saviour's breast.

HYMN CCXXXVI. Common Metre. The Coll. J.
Lord's day Morning.

1 TO day God bids the faithful rest,
  To day he show'rs his grace;
"Seek ye my face," thy Lord hath said
  Lord, we will seek thy face.

2 Come, let us leave the things of earth,
  With God's assembly join;
Lo! Heaven descends to welcome man,
  To taste the things divine!

3 We come, dear Saviour, lo! we come,
  Lord of our life and soul;
We come diseas'd, and faint, and sick;
  Be pleas'd to make us whole.

4 We thirst, and fly to thee, O LORD,
  Thou fountain-head of good;
Filthy we come, and all unclean;
  O cleanse us in thy blood.

5 O may

5 O may we please our God to day,
   May that be all our care!
 Give, Lord, thy grace, lest evil thoughts
   Should mingle in our pray'r,

6 Amidst th' assembly of thy saints
   Let us be faithful found;
 And let us join in humble pray'r,
   And in thy praise abound.

7 Let thy good Spirit help our souls,
   With faith thy word to hear;
 Be with us in thy temple, LORD,
   And let us find thee near.

CCXXXVII. Common Metre. (Pf. xix.) *J.*

Lord's day Morning.

1 BEHOLD the morning sun.
   Begins his glorious way;
 His beams through all the nations run,
   And life and light convey.

2 But where the gospel comes,
   It spreads diviner light;
 It calls dead sinners from their tombs,
   And gives the blind their sight.

3 How perfect is thy word!
   And all thy judgements just;

For

For ever sure thy promise, LORD,
   And men securely trust.

4 My gracious GOD, how plain
   Are thy directions giv'n!
O may I never read in vain,
   But find the path to heav'n!

CCXXXVIII. Common Metre. (Pf. iv. Dr. Watts) J.

Evening.

LORD, thou wilt hear me when I pray
   I am for ever thine;
I fear before thee all the day,
   Nor would I dare to sin.

2 And while I rest my weary head,
   From cares and bus'ness free,
'Tis sweet conversing on my bed,
   With my own heart and thee.

3 I pay this evening sacrifice;
   And when my work is done,
Great God, my faith and hope relies,
   Upon thy grace alone.

4 Thus with my thoughts compos'd to peace
   I'll give mine eyes to sleep;
Thy hand in safety keeps my days,
   And will my slumbers keep.

HYMN CCXXXIX. Com. Metre. Newport Coll. J.
Lord's day Morning.

1 LORD haſt thou ſuffer'd me to ſee
    Another of thy days!
O fill my heart with love to thee,
    And tune my lips to praiſe!

2 Within thy lower courts of grace,
    Let me with pleaſure ſtay;
And let a ſmile from Jeſus' face,
    Chaſe all my doubts away.

3 Diſplay the riches of thy grace,
    My broken heart to cheer:
And ſhew thy reconciled face
    To all thy people here.

4 As in the ancient days O Lord,
    Thy glorious trophies ſpread;
Gird on thy all victorious ſword,
    And fill thy foes with dread.

5 Let ev'ry hard'ned ſinner here,
    Feel that thy pow'r abounds;
Each broken heart with comforts cheer,
    And heal their bleeding wounds

6 Deſcend, O ſweet celeſtial dove,
    With all thy quick'ning pow'rs!
                    Cauſe

Cause now a dear Redeemer's love,
    T' enflame and quicken ours.

HYMN CCXL. Common Metre. Newport Coll. J.

Lord's day Evening.

1 NOW Lord, another of thy days,
    I have on earth enjoy'd,
  But ah, how little to thy praise,
    My heart has been employ'd!

2 Tho' I have heard thy holy word,
    And in thy worship join'd,
  Alas, how little of it, Lord,
    Remains upon my mind!

3 Wast thou to call me to account,
    What I have gain'd this day;
  How low the product would amount,
    I tremble, Lord to say!

4 Much like the barren heath am I,
    Tho' oft refresh'd with rain,
  Still it continues hard and dry,
    And fruitless doth remain.

5 For Jesus' sake my fruitlesness,
    Remember, Lord no more;
  And whilst my guilt I here confess,
    Purge out my heinous score.

6 And e'er my soul shall be undrest,
   To take its last remove;
 O fit me for that glorious rest
   Thou hast prepar'd above.

HYMN CCXLI. Short Metre. Rippon's Coll. J.

A Morning Hymn.

1 SEE how the mounting sun,
   Pursues his shining way;
 And wide proclaims his maker's praise,
   With every bright'ning ray.

2 Thus would my rising soul,
   Its heavenly parent sing;
 And to its great original,
   The humble tribute bring.

3 Serene I laid me down,
   Beneath his guardian care;
 I slept, and I awoke, and found,
   My kind preserver near!

4 Thus does thine arm support,
   This weak defenceless frame;
 But whence these favours, Lord, to me,
   All worthless as I am?

5 Oh! how shall I repay
   The bounties of my God,

This feeble spirit pants beneath,
   The pleasing, painful load.

6 Dear Saviour, to thy cross,
   I bring my sacrifice;
Ting'd with thy blood it shall ascend,
   With fragrance to the skies.

7 My life I would anew,
   Devote, O LORD, to thee;
And, in thy service, I would spend,
   A long eternity.

HYMN CCXLII. Common Metre. Rippon's Coll. *J.*
An Evening Hymn.

1 NOW from the altar of our hearts,
   Let flames of love arise;
Assist us, LORD, to offer up
   Our evening sacrifice.

2 Minutes and mercies multiply'd,
   Have made up all this day;
Minutes came quick, but mercies were
   More swift and free than they.

3 New time, new favour, and new joys,
   Do a new song require,
'Till we shall praise thee as we would,
   Accept our hearts desire.

4 LORD of our days, whose hand hath set
   New time upon our score;
Thee may we praise for all our time,
   When time shall be no more.

HYMN CCXLIII. Long Metre. Bp. Ken.   *J.*

Evening.

GLORY to thee, my God, this night,
For all the blessings of the light;
Keep me, O keep me, King of kings,
Under thine own Almighty wings.

2 Forgive me, Lord, for thy dear Son,
What ever ill this day I've done;
That, with the world, myself and thee,
I, ere I sleep, at peace may be.

3 Teach me to live, that I may dread.
The grave as little as my bed;
Teach me to die, that so I may,
Triumphing rise at the last day.

4 O may my soul on thee repose,
And with sweet sleep my eye-lids close;
Sleep that may me more vig'rous make,
To serve my God when I awake.

5 Let my blest guardian, while I sleep,
Close to my bed his vigils keep;

FAMILY WORSHIP.

Let no vain dreams disturb my rest,
No powers of darkness me molest.

Praise God, from whom all blessings flow
Praise him, all creatures here below;
Praise him above, ye heav'nly host;
Praise Father, Son, and Holy Ghost.

HYMN CCXLIV. Long Metre. The Coll. J.

Morning.

AWAKE, my soul, and with the sun
Thy daily stage of duty run;
Shake off dull sloth, and early rise,
To pay thy morning sacrifice.

Redeem thy misspent time that's past,
Live this day as if 'twere thy last;
T' improve thy talents take due care,
'Gainst the great day thyself prepare.

Let all thy converse be sincere,
Thy conscience as the noon day clear;
Think how th' all seeing God thy ways
And all thy secret thoughts surveys.

Glory to God, who safe hath kept,
And hath refresh'd me while I slept;
Grant Lord when I from death shall wake,
I may of endless life partake.

5 Direct, controul, suggest this day,
All I design, or do, or say;
That all my pow'rs, with all their might
In thy sole glory may unite.

6 Praise God from whom all blessings flow
Praise him all creatures here below;
Praise him above ye Heav'nly host;
Praise Father, Son, and Holy Ghost.

HYMN CCXLV. Common Metre. Cennick. *J*

Lord's day Evening.

WHEN, O dear Jesus, when shall I
Behold thee all serene;
Blest in perpetual sabbath day,
Without a veil between?

2 Assist me while I wander here,
Amidst a world of cares;
Incline my heart to pray with love,
And then accept my pray'rs.

3 Release my soul from ev'ry chain,
No more hell's captive led;
And pardon a repenting child,
For whom the Saviour bled.

4 Spare me, O God, O spare the soul,
That gives itself to thee;

Take

Take all that I possess below,
  And give thyself to me.

5 Thy Spirit, O my Father, give,
  To be my guide and friend;
To light my way to ceaseless joys!
  Where Sabbaths never end.

HYMN CCXLVI. Long Metre. Dr. Watts. *J.*

Morning or Evening.

1 MY God, how endless is thy love!
    Thy gifts are ev'ry ev'ning new
  And morning mercies from above
    Gently distil like early dew.

2 Thou spread'st the curtains of the night,
    Great guardian of my sleeping hours
  Thy sov'reign word restores the light,
    And quickens all my drowsy pow'rs

2 I yield my pow'rs to thy command;
    To thee I consecrate my days;
  Perpetual blessings from thine hand,
    Demand perpetual songs of praise.

HYMN CCXLVII. Common Metre. Dr. Watts. *A.*

For the Morning.

1 ONCE more, my soul, the rising day
    Salutes thy waking eyes;

Once more, my voice, thy tribute pay,
  To him that rules the skies.

2 Night unto night his name repeats,
  The day renews the sound,
Wide as the heav'n on which he sits,
  To turn the seasons round.

3 'Tis he supports my mortal frame;
  My tongue shall speak his praise;
My sins would rouse his wrath to flame,
  And yet his wrath delays.

4 A thousand wretched souls are fled,
  Since the last setting sun,
And yet thou length'nest out my thread
  And yet my moments run.

5 Dear God, let all my hours be thine,
  Whilst I enjoy the light;
Then shall my sun in smiles decline,
  And bring a pleasant night.

HYMN CCXLVIII. *Common Metre. Dr. Watts. A.*
Morning or Evening.

1 HOSANNA with a cheerful sound,
  To God's upholding hand;
Ten thousand snares attend us round,
  And yet secure we stand.

2 That was a moſt amazing pow'r,
   That rais'd us with a word,
And ev'ry day, and ev'ry hour,
   We lean upon the Lord.

3 The ev'ning reſts our weary head,
   And angels guard the room;
We wake, and we admire the bed,
   That was not made our tomb.

4 The riſing morning can't aſſure,
   That we ſhall end the day;
For death ſtands ready at the door
   To take our lives away.

5 Our breath is forfeited by ſin
   To God's avenging law;
We own thy grace, immortal King,
   In ev'ry gaſp we draw.

6 God is our ſun, whoſe daily light,
   Our joy and ſafety brings;
Our feeble fleſh lies ſafe at night
   Beneath his ſhady wings.

HYMN CCXLIX. Common Metre. The Coll. *A.*
Faith the Gift of God.

1 HAIL, Alpha and Omega, hail!
   Author of all our faith,

  The finisher of all our hopes,
    The truth, the life, the path.

2 Hail, first and last, the morning star,
  In whom we live and move;
Increase our little spark of faith,
  And purify our love.

3 Let that belief which Jesus taught,
  Be treasur'd in our breast;
The evidence of unseen joys,
  The substance of our rest.

4 O let us go from strength to strength,
  From grace to greater grace,
From one degree of faith to more,
  Till we behold thy face.

HYMN CCL. Common Metre. Lyric Poems.
Omnipotent God.

1 THE Lord! how fearful is his name
  How wide is his command?
Nature with all her moving frame,
  Rest on his mighty hand.

2 Immortal glory forms his throne,
  And light his awful robe;
Whilst with a smile or with a frown,
  He manages the globe.

3 A word of his Almighty breath,
    Can swell or sink the seas;
 Build the vast empires of the earth,
    Or break them as he please.

4 Adoring angels round him fall,
    In all their shining forms,
 His sovereign eye looks thro' them all
    And pities mortal worms.

5 Now let the Lord for ever reign,
    And sway us as he will,
 Sick, or in health, in ease, or pain,
    We are his fav'rites still.

HYMN CCLI. Common Metre. Dr. Watts. *A.*
Tribulation below.

1 LORD, what a wretched land is this
    That yields us no supply,
 No cheering fruits, no wholesome trees
    No streams of living joy?

2 But pricking thorns thro' all the ground,
    And mortal poisons grow;
 And all the rivers that are found,
    With dang'rous water flow.

3 Yet the dear path to thine abode,
    Lies thro' this horrid land:

LORD!

Lord! we would keep the heav'nly road
And run at thy command.

4 Our souls shall tread the desert thro'
With undiverted feet:
And faith and flaming zeal subdue,
The terrors that we meet.

5 Our journey is a thorny maze,
But we march upward still;
Forget these troubles of the ways,
And reach at Zion's Hill.

HYMN CCLII. Long Metre. Dr. Watts.

Seeking the Lord.

1 OFTEN I seek my Lord by night;
Jesus, my love, my soul's delight
With warm desire and restless thought,
I seek him oft, but find him not.

2 Then I arise and search the street,
Till I my Lord, my Saviour meet;
I ask the watchman of the night,
" Where did you see my soul's delight.'

3 Sometimes I find him in my way,
Directed by a heav'nly ray;
I leap for joy to see his face,
And hold him fast in my embrace,

4 He

4 He gives me there his bleeding heart,
  Pierc'd for my sins with deadly smart;
  I give my soul to him, and there,
  Our loves there mutual tokens share.

5 I charge you all, ye earthly toys;
  Approach not to disturb my joys;
  Nor sin nor hell come near my heart,
  Nor cause my Saviour to depart.

HYMN CCLIII. Long Metre. Newport Coll. *A*
Divine use of Musick.

WE sing to thee, whose wisdom form'd
    The curious organ of the ear;
  And thou who gav'st us voices, Lord,
    Our grateful songs in kindness hear.

2 We'll joy in God who is the spring,
    Of lawful joy and harmless mirth;
  Whose boundless love is fitly call'd,
    The harmony of heav'n and earth.

3 Those praises, dearest Lord, aloud,
    Our humble sonnets shall rehearse:
  Which rightly tun'd, are rightly stil'd,
    The musick of the universe.

4 And whilst we sing; we'll consecrate,
    That too, too much profaned art,

By

By off'ring up with ev'ry tongue,
    In ev'ry song a flaming heart.

5 We'll hallow pleasure and redeem,
    From vulgar use our precious voice
Those lips which wantonly have sung,
    Shall serve our turn for nobler joys

HYMN CCLIV. Long Metre. Newport Coll. *A.*

A Morning Hymn.

1 AWAKE my soul, awake mine eyes,
    Awake, my drowsy faculties:
Awake and see the new-born light,
Spring from the darksome womb of night.

2 Look up and see the unwearied sun;
Already has his race begun,
The pretty lark is mounted high,
And sings his matins in the sky.

3 Arise my soul and thou my voice,
In early songs of praise rejoice,
O great creator, Heav'nly King,
Thy praises ever let me sing.

4 Thy power has made, thy goodness kept
This fenceless body while I slept:
Yet one night more hast thou kept me,
From all the pow'rs of darkness free.

5 O

5 O keep my heart from sin secure,
My life unblameable and pure;
That when the last of days shall come;
I chearfully may meet my doom.

HYMN CCLV. Long Metre. Newport Coll. A.

An Evening Hymn.

Sleep, downy sleep, come, close mine eyes,
Tir'd with beholding vanities.
Welcome sweet sleep and chase away,
The toils and follies of the day.

2 On thy soft bosom, will I lie,
Forget the world, and learn to die,
O Israel's watchful shepherd spread,
Thy guardian angels round my bed.

3 Let not the spirits of the air,
While I lie slumb'ring me insnare;
But guard thy suppliant free from harm
Claspt in thine everlasting arm.

4 Clouds and thick darkness are thy throne
Thy wonderful pavilion,
O dart from thence one heav'nly ray,
And then my midnight shall be day.

5 Thus when the morn in crimson dress,
Break through the windows of the east,

My thankful hymns of praise shall rise,
Like incense of the sacrifice.

HYMN CCLVI. Long Metre. Stennett.　　A.

The Christian Honourable.

1 NOT all the nobles of the earth,
　Who boast the honors of their birth
Such real dignity can claim,
As those who bear the christian name,

2 To them the privilege is giv'n,
To be the sons and heirs of Heav'n,
Sons of the GOD who reigns on high,
And heirs of joys beyond the sky.

3 On them a happy chosen race,
Their father pours his richest grace:
To them his counsels he imparts,
And stamps his Image on their hearts.

4 Their Infant cries, their tender age,
His pity and his love engage:
He clasps them in his arms and there,
Secures them with parental care.

5 His will he makes them early know,
And teaches their young feet to go;
Whispers instruction to their minds,
And on their hearts his precepts binds.

CCLVII. Long Metre. (Pf. li.) A.
Depravity of Nature.

1 LORD I am vile, conceiv'd in sin,
  And born unholy and unclean;
  Sprung from the man whose guilty fall,
  Corrupts the race, and taints us all.

2 Soon as we draw our infant breath,
  The seeds of sin grow up for death;
  Thy law demands a perfect heart;
  But we're defil'd in ev'ry part.

3 Great God create my heart anew,
  And form my spirit pure and true:
  O make me wise, betimes, to spy,
  My danger and my remedy.

4 Behold I fall before thy face,
  My only refuge is thy grace:
  No outward forms can make me clean,
  The leprosy lies deep within.

5 No bleeding bird, nor bleeding beast,
  Nor hyssop branch, nor sprinkling priest
  Nor running brook, nor flood, nor sea,
  Can wash the dismal stain away.

HYMN CCLVIII. Short Metre. Dr. Watts. A.
Christ's presence desirable.

1 MY God, my life, my love;
 To thee, to thee I call;
I cannot live if thou remove,
 For thou art all in all.

2 (Thy shining grace can cheer
 This dungeon where I dwell;
'Tis paradise when thou art here;
 If thou depart, 'tis hell.)

3 The smilings of thy face,
 How amiable they are!
'Tis heaven to rest in thine embrace,
 And no where else but there.)

4 (To thee, and thee alone,
 The angels owe their bliss;
They sit around thy gracious throne
 And dwell where Jesus is.)

5 Nor earth, nor all the sky,
 Can one delight afford;
No, not a drop of real joy,
 Without thy presence, Lord.

HYMN CCLIX. Long Metre. The Coll. A.
The believer Christ's property.

1 AND is it yet dear Lord, a doubt,
    If in my breast thou reign'st alone
O find the lurking rival out,
    And drag the traitor from the throne

2 Would earth's delusive trifling charms
    Assume a pow'r above thy name?
Stab each usurper in my arms,
    And vindicate thy rightful claim.

3 By purchase, duty, ev'ry tie,
    Yea choice itself, Lord, I am thine;
Maintain thy right, or let me die,
    Ere from thy love my soul decline.

4 If my unsteady heart wou'd rove,
    (And well thou know'st its treach'rous frame,)
If ought below, or ought above,
    Wou'd share or quench the sacred flame;

5 Chace the curs'd object from my soul,
    Thence, thence the twining mischief tear;

Reign thou the sovereign of the whole
Be LORD of ev'ry motion there.

HYMN CCLX. Twice 5 & 11. The Coll.   J.

Adoring Jesus.

1 O come let us join,
　　Together combine,
To praise our dear Saviour, our Master
　　divine.

2 He worthy is blest
　　By spirits at rest,
Who once in this desert his Godhead con-
　　fess'd.

3 The prophets who told
　　His suff'rings of old,
Sing now sweet thanksgivings on psalt'ries
　　of gold.

4 The fathers to whom
　　He shew'd he would come,
Now in his pavilion take up their long
　　home.

5 The spirits of men,
　　Who for him were slain,
From Abel the righteous, share now in his
　　reign.

6 The

WORSHIP.

5 The apostles who stood,
 Resisting to blood
For Jesus' gospel, rejoice in their God.

6 O church of the Lamb
 Here met, do the same,
With saints and with angels bless Jesus's name.

7 My soul bear a part,
 For ransom'd thou art
By Jesus' blood-shedding, his burial and smart.

8 To him that was slain,
 The scorn'd Nazarene,
Be glory and honour; let all say Amen.

HYMN CCLXI. Twice 5 & 11. The Coll. *J.*
Faith's claim.

ALL ye that pass by
 To Jesus draw nigh,
To you is it nothing that Jesus shou'd die?
 Your ransom and peace,
 Your surety he is,
Come see if there ever was sorrow like his.

 For what you have done
 His blood must atone;

The

The father has punish'd for you his dear
    Son;
  He answer'd for all,
  O come at his call,
And low at his cross with astonishment fall.

3 For you and for me
  He pray'd on the tree;
The pray'r is accepted, the sinner set free;
  That sinner am I,
  Who on JESUS rely,
And come for the pardon GOD will not deny

4 My pardon I claim,
  For a sinner I am,
A sinner believing in JESUS' name.
  He purchas'd the grace
  Which now I embrace,
O Father, thou know'st he has dy'd in my
    place.

5 His death is my plea,
  My Advocate see,
And here the blood speak, that has
    answer'd for me;
  Acquitted I was,

When

WORSHIP.

When he bled on the cross,
And by losing his life he has carry'd my
cause.

HYMN CCLXII.
Blessings of the Gospel.

1 O Jesus, our Lord,
   Thy name be ador'd,
For all the rich blessings convey'd by thy
word.

2 In spirit we trace
   Thy wonders of grace,
And cheerfully join in a concert of praise.

3 The antient of days
   His glory displays;
And shines on his chosen with quick'ning
rays.

4 The trumpet of God
   Is sounding aloud,
The language of mercy--salvation thro'
blood.

5 Thrice happy are they
   That hear and obey,
And share in the blessings of this gospel
day.

The

6 The people who know
  The Saviour below,
With burning affection to worship him
    glow.

7 This blessing be mine,
  Thro' favour divine;
But O, my Redeemer, the glory be thine.

    HYMN CCLXIII. *Twice 6 & 4, thrice 6 & 4.*
        The Coll.   J.
      At Opening worship.

1 COME, thou Almighty King,
   Help us thy name to sing,
   Help us to praise!
Father all glorious,
O'er all victorious,
Come, and reign over us,
   ANTIENT OF DAYS.

2 JESUS, our LORD, arise,
Scatter our enemies,
   And make them fall!
Let thine Almighty aid
Our sure defence be made,
Our souls on thee be stay'd:
   LORD, hear our call!

                3 Come

3 Come, thou incarnate word,
  Gird on thy mighty fword,
    Our pray'r attend!
  Come! and thy people blefs,
  And give thy word fuccefs;
  Spirit of holinefs
    On us defcend!

4 Come, holy comforter,
  Thy facred witnefs bear
    In this glad hour!
  Thou who Almighty art,
  Now rule in ev'ry heart,
  And ne'er from us depart,
    Spirit of pow'r!

5 To thee great one in three,
  Eternal praifes be,
    Hence---evermore!
  His fov'reign Majefty
  May we in glory fee,
  And to eternity,
    Love and adore.

HYMN CCLXIV. twice 6, 8 & 4, D Oliver. *J.*
The Covenant God.

1 THE God of Abra'm praife,
    Who reigns enthron'd above;

Ancient

Ancient of everlasting days,
    And GOD of love;
Jehovah great I AM!
    By earth and Heaven confess'd,
I bow and bless the sacred name,
    For ever bless'd.

2 The GOD of Abra'm praise,
    At whose supreme command,
From earth I rise, and seek the joys
    At his right hand.
I'd all on earth forsake,
    Its wisdom, Fame and power;
And him my only portion make,
    My shield and tower.

3 The GOD of Abra'm praise,
    Whose all sufficient grace
Shall guide me all my happy days,
    In all his ways:
He calls a worm his friend!
    He calls himself my GOD!
And he shall save me to the end,
    Thro' JESUS' blood.

4 He by himself hath sworn,
    I on his oath depend,

I shall, on eagles wings up-borne,
   To Heaven ascend.
I shall behold his face,
   I shall his power adore;
And sing the wonders of his grace,
   For evermore?

PART THE SECOND.

5 Tho' nature's strength decay,
   And earth and hell withstand;
To Canaan's bounds I urge my way,
   At God's command:
The wat'ry deep I pass,
   With JESUS in my view,
And thro' the howling wilderness
   My way pursue.

6 The goodly land I see,
   With peace and plenty blest;
The land of sacred liberty,
   And endless rest.
There milk and honey flow,
   And oil and wine abound;
The trees of life forever grow,
   With mercy crown'd.

7 There dwells the LORD our King,
   The LORD our righteousness;
                   Triumphant

Triumphant o'er the world and sin,
    The Prince of peace.
On Zion's sacred height,
    His Kingdom still maintains;
And glorious, with his saints in light,
    For ever reigns.

8 The ransom'd nations bow,
    Before the Saviour's face,
And at his feet their crowns they throw,
    O'erwhelm'd with grace:
He shews his prints of love,
    They kindle to a flame,
And sound thro' all the worlds above,
    "The slaughter'd Lamb."

9 The whole triumphant host
    Give thanks to GOD on high:
"Hail Father, Son, and Holy Ghost!"
    They ever cry.
Hail Abra'm's God and mine,
    I join the Heavenly lays:
All might and majesty are thine,
    And endless praise.

HYMN

NEW-YEAR'S DAY.

HYMN CCLXV. Four 6, and twice 8. The Coll. J.
For New Year's Day.

1 THE Lord of earth and sky,
  The God of ages praise!
Who reigns enthron'd on high,
  Ancient of endless days;
Who lengthens out our trial here,
And spares us yet another year.

2 Barren and wither'd trees,
  We cumber'd long the ground;
No fruit of holiness
  On our dead souls was found;
Yet did he us in mercy spare
  Another, and another year.

3 When justice bar'd the sword,
  To cut the fig-tree down,
The pity of our Lord
  Cry'd, "Let it still alone:"
The Father mild inclin'd his ear,
  And spar'd us yet another year.

4 Jesus, thy speaking Blood
  From God obtain'd the grace,
Who therefore hath bestow'd
  On us a longer space:

5 Thou

Thou didst in our behalf appear,
And lo! we see another year.

5 Then dig about our root,
    Break up our fallow ground,
And let our gracious fruit
    To thy great praise abound.
O let us all thy praise declare,
And fruit unto perfection bear.

HYMN CCLXVI. Four 6, and twice 8. The Cell. *J.*

The Barren Fig-Tree.

1 THE Church a garden is,
    In which believers stand,
Like ornamental trees,
    Planted by God's own hand,
His Spirit waters all their roots,
And every branch abounds with fruit.

2 But other trees there are
    In this inclosure grow,
Which tho' they promise fair,
    Have only leaves to shew;
No fruits of grace are on them found,
They are but cumb'rers of the ground.

3 The under-gard'ner grieves,
    In vain his strength he spends,

For

NEW YEAR'S DAY.

For heaps of useless leaves,
   Affords him small amends:
He hears the Lord his will make known,
   To cut the barren fig-tree down.

4 How difficult his post!
   What pangs his bowels move!
To find his wishes crost,
   His efforts useless prove,
His last relief is earnest pray'r,
   Lord spare them yet another year.

5 Spare them and let me try
   What further means may do;
I'll fresh manure apply,
   My diging I'll renew:
Who knows, but yet they fruit may yield,
   If not---'tis just they must be fell'd.

6 If under means of grace
   No fruit of grace appear,
It is a dreadful case,
   Tho' God may long forbear;
At length he'll strike the threaten'd blow
   And lay the barren fig-tree low.

HYMN

HYMN CCLXVII Four 6 and twice 8 The Coll. *J.*
Rejoice. Phill. iv iv.

1 REJOICE the Lord is King,
 Your God and King adore;
Mortals give thanks, and sing,
 And triumph evermore:
Lift up your hearts lift up your voice;
 Rejoice, again I say, rejoice.

2 Jesus the Saviour reigns,
 The God of truth and love;
When he had purg'd our stains,
 He took his seat above:
Lift up your hearts, &c.

3 His kingdom cannot fail,
 He rules o'er earth and heav'n;
The keys of death and hell
 Are to our Jesus giv'n:
Lift up your hearts, &c.

4 He sits at God's right hand,
 Till all his foes submit
And bow to his command,
 And fall beneath his feet:
Lift up your hearts, &c.

5 He all his foes shall quell,
 Shall all our sins destroy;

And

And every bosom swell
  With pure seraphic joy:
Lift up your hearts, &c.

6 Rejoice in glorious hope,
    Jesus the judge shall come,
  And take his servants up
    To their eternal home:
  We soon shall hear th' arch angel's voice,
  The trump of God shall sound, rejoice.

HYMN CCLXVIII. Four 6 and twice 8 Cowper. J.
The Ceremonial Law.

ISRAEL in ancient days,
    Not only had a view
  Of Sinai in a blaze,
    But learn'd the gospel too:
  The types and figures were a glass,
  In which they saw the Saviour's face.

The Paschal sacrifice,
And blood besprinkled door;
Seen with enlighten'd eyes,
And once apply'd with power,
Would teach the need of other blood,
To reconcile an angry God.

H 2   3 The

3 The Lamb, the dove set forth,
   His perfect innocence,
   Whose blood of matchless worth,
   Should be the soul's defence,
   For he who can for sin atone,
   Must have no failing of his own.

4 The scape goat on his head,
   The people's trespass bore,
   And to the desert led,
   Was to be seen no more:
   In him our surety seemed to say,
   " Behold I bear your sins away."

5 Dipt in his fellows blood,
   The living bird went free;
   The type well understood,
   Express'd the sinner's plea;
   Described a guilty soul enlarg'd,
   And by a Saviour's death discharg'd.

6 Jesus I love to trace
   Throughout the sacred page,
   The footsteps of thy grace,
   The same in every age:
   O grant that I may faithful be,
   To clearer light, vouchsaf'd to me.

CCLX

CCLXIX. 4 of 6 & 2 of 8. (Pf. cxxi.) . A.

God our Support.

UPward I lift mine eyes;
    From God is all my aid;
The God that built the fkies.
And earth and nature made:
" God is the tower to which I fly,
" His grace is nigh in ev'ry hour.

My feet fhall never flide,
And fall in fatal fnares,
Since God my guard and guide,
Defends me from my fears.
" Thofe wakeful eyes that never fleep,
" Shall Ifr'el keep when dangers rife.

Haft thou not giv'n thy word,
To fave my foul from death?
And I can truft my Lord,
To keep my mortal breath:
" I'll go and come nor fear to die,
" Till from on high thou call me home.

CCLXX. (Pf. cxxxvi)

Power and Grace.

GIVE thanks to God moft high,
    The univerfal Lord;

POWER AND GRACE.

  The sovereign King of Kings,
  And be his grace ador'd.
    " His pow'er and grace,
    " Are still the same;
    " And let his name
    " have endless praise.

2 How mighty is his hand!
  What wonders hath he done!
  He form'd the earth and seas,
  And spreads the Heav'ns alone.
    " Thy mercy, Lord,
    " Shall still endure;
    " And ever sure,"
    " Abides thy word.

3 His wisdom fram'd the sun,
  To crown the day with light;
  The moon and twinkling stars,
  To chear the darksome night.
    " His pow'r and grace,
    " Are still the same;
    " And let his name
    " Have endless praise.

CCLXXI. (Pf. cxlviii.)

Praife to God from all creatures.

YE tribes of Adam join,
With Heav'n and earth and feas,
And offer notes divine,
To your Creator's praife.
 Ye holy throng
 Of angels bright,
 In worlds of light
 Begin the fong.

Thou fun, with dazzling rays,
And moon that rules the night,
Shine to your Maker's praife,
With ftars of twinkling light.
 His pow'r declare,
 Ye floods on high,
 And clouds that fly,
 In empty air.

The fhining world above,
In glorious order ftand,
Or in fwift courfes move,
By his fupreme command.
 He fpake the word
 And all their frame

From nothing came,
To praise the Lord.

HYMN CCLXXII. P. M. 4 of 6 & 4 of 4. Dr. Watts. *A.*
Majesty of Christ.

1 WITH cheerful voice I sing,
    The titles of my LORD,
And borrow all the names
Of honor from his word;
  " Nature and art
  " Can ne'er supply
  " Sufficient forms
  " Of Majesty.

2 In JESUS we behold
His Father's glorious face,
Shining forever bright
With mild and lovely rays.
  " Th' eternal GOD's
  " Eternal Son
  " Inherits, and
  " Partakes the throne.

3 Immense compassion reigns
In our Immanuel's heart,
When he descends to act
A Mediator's part.

> He is a friend
> And brother too;
> Divinely kind
> Divinely true.

HYMN CCLXXIII. Four 6 & 2, 8. B. Francis. J.
On Opening a Place of Worship.

1 IN sweet exalted strains
  The King of glory praise;
 Oe'r Heaven and earth he reigns,
  Thro' everlasting days:
He with a nod the world controuls,
Sustains or sinks the distant poles.

2 To earth he bends his throne,
  His throne of grace divine;
 Wide is his bounty known,
  And wide his glories shine:
Fair Salem, still his chosen rest,
Is with his smiles and presence blest.

3 Then, King of glory come,
  And with thy favour crown
 This temple as thy dome,
  This people as thy own:
Beneath this roof, O deign to show,
How GOD can dwell with men below.

4 Here, may thine ears attend
    Our interceding cries,
And grateful praise ascend
    All fragrant to the skies:
Here may thy word melodious sound,
And spread celestial joys around.

5 Here may th' attentive throng
    Imbibe thy truth and love,
And converts join the song
    Of Seraphim above,
And willing crouds surround thy board
With sacred joy and sweet accord.

6 Here may our unborn sons
    And daughters sound thy praise,
And shine like polish'd stones,
    Thro' long succeeding days;
Here, LORD, display thy saving power,
While temples stand, and men adore.

HYMN CCLXXIV. Four 6 & twice 8. Hart. *J*
On Baptism.

1 REPENT and be baptis'd,
    Saith your redeeming LORD,
Ye all are now appris'd
    That 'tis your Saviour's word,
              Arise

Arise, arise without delay,
And Christ's divine commands obey.

2 Come ye believing train,
    No more this truth withstand,
No longer think it vain
    T' obey your LORD's command:
But haste, arise, without delay,
And be baptis'd in JESUS' way.

3 JESUS, thou Prince of peace,
    To thy great name we pray,
Make the converted race,
    Thine ordinance obey:
O may thy love their souls o'ercome
And draw them to thy liquid tomb.

HYMN CCLXXV 4 of 6 and 2 of 8. The Coll. A.
Gospel Trumpet.

1 BLOW ye the trumpet, blow,
    The gladly solemn sound,
Let all the nation know,
    To earth's remotest bound
The year of Jubilee is come;
Return, ye ransom'd sinners, home.

Exalt the Son of God
The All atoning Lamb;

Redemption in his blood
   To all the world proclaim:
   The year of Jubilee is come,
   Return ye ransom'd sinners, home.

3 Ye who have sold for nought
   Your heritage above;
   Come take it back unbought,
   The gift of JESUS' love;
   The year of Jubilee, is come,
   Return, ye ransom'd sinners, home.

4 The gospel trumpet sounds;
   Let all the nation hear
   And earth's remotest bounds
   Before the throne appear
   The year of Jubilee is come,
   Return ye ransom'd sinners home.

HYMN CCLXXVI. 4 of 6, and 2 of 8 Rippon's Coll. A

Christ's Resurrection.

1 AWAKE, our drowsy Souls,
      Shake off each slothful band,
   The wonders of this day
      Our noblest songs demand,
   Auspicious morn! thy blissful rays,
      Bright seraphs hail in song of praise.

2 At thy approaching dawn,
   Reluctant death resign'd
The glorious Prince of life,
   Her dark domains confin'd
Th' angelic host around him bends,
   And 'midst their shouts, the God as-
                                  (cends.
3 All hail, triumphant Lord,
   Heaven with Hosannas rings;
While earth, in humbler strains,
   Thy praise responsive sings:
Worthy art thou, who once was slain,
   Through endless years to live and reign.

Make bare thy potent arm,
   And wing th' unerring dart,
With salutary pangs,
   To each rebellious heart:
Then dying souls for life shall sue,
   Numerous as drops of morning dew.

HYMN CCLXXVII. 7 & 6, 7 & 6, 7 & 8, 7 & 6.
   The poor sinner.   The Coll.   J.

1 GOD of my salvation, hear,
      And help me to believe;
  Simply do I now draw near,
      Thy blessing to receive:

Full of guilt, alas! I am,
  But to thy wounds for refuge flee;
Friend of sinners, spotless Lamb,
  Thy blood was shed for me.

2 Nothing have I, LORD, to pay,
  Nor can thy grace procure;
Empty send me not away,
  For I, thou know'st, am poor;
Dust and ashes is my name,
  My all is sin and misery:
Friend of sinners, spotless Lamb,
  Thy blood was shed for me.

3 Without money, without price,
  I come thy love to buy;
From myself I turn my eyes,
  The chief of sinners, I:
Take, O take me, as I am,
  And let me lose myself in thee;
Friend of sinners, spotless Lamb,
  Thy blood was shed for me.

HYMN CCLXXVIII. The Coll.   J.
The same.

1 JESU, friend of sinners, hear,
  Yet once again I pray;

From

The POOR SINNER.

From my debt of sin set clear,
   For I have nought to pay.
Speak, O speak the kind release!
   A poor backsliding soul restore;
Love me freely, seal my peace,
   And bid me sin no more.

Sin's deceitfulness hath spread
   An hardness o'er my heart;
But if thou thy Spirit shed,
   The stony shall depart:
Shed thy love thy tenderness,
   And let me feel thy soft'ning pow'r;
Love me freely, seal my peace,
   And bid me sin no more.

For this only thing I pray,
   And this will I require,
Take the love of sin away,
   Take ev'ry vain desire!
Perfect me in holiness,
   Thine image to my soul restore;
Love me freely seal my peace,
   And bid me sin no more.

HYMN

BACKSLIDER'S PRAYER.

HYMN CCLXXIX. 7 & 6, 7 & 6, 7 & 8, 7 & 6,
Rippon's Coll.   J.

The backslider's prayer.

1 JESUS, let thy pitying eye
    Call back a wand'ring sheep;
False to thee, like Peter, I
    Would fain like Peter weep;
Let me be by grace restor'd,
    On me be all its freeness shewn;
Turn and look upon me, LORD,
    And break my heart of stone.

2 Saviour prince, enthron'd above,
Repentance to impart,
    Give me thro' thy dying love,
The humble contrite heart;
    Give, what I have long implor'd,
A portion of thy love unknown;
    Turn and look upon me LORD,
And break my heart of stone.

3 See me, Saviour, from above,
    Nor suffer me to die;
Life, and happiness, and love,
    Drop from thy gracious eye:
Speak the reconciling word
    And let thy mercy melt me down;
                    Turn

BACKSLIDER'S PRAYER.

 Turn and look upon me, LORD,
  And break my heart of stone.

4 Look as when thy pitying eye,
  Was clos'd that we might live;
 Father (at the point to die,
  My Saviour gasp'd) "Forgive!"
 Surely with that dying word,
  He turns, and looks, and cries, "'tis done!"
 O! my loving, bleeding LORD,
  This breaks my heart of stone.

HYMN CCLXXX. *The same.*   J.

1 HEAR me, O Redeemer, hear,
  My humble suit receive;
 While I all my wants declare,
  And how unhelp'd I grieve;
 JESUS master I have sinn'd,
  My soul hath greatly gone astray,
 Dear Redeemer be my friend,
  And bring me on my way.

2 I am hungry all my cry,
  Is for the living bread;
 Neither have I ought to buy,
  Nor any thing to plead:

Helpless begging at the door,
  I ask the food that came from heav'n,
See me needy, lost, and poor,
  And let relief be giv'n.

3 Hidden manna, Lord, reveal,
  For this behold I pant;
Let thine ears consider well
  The voice of my complaint;
Let the tree of life relieve
  A weary traveller near to die;
May it please thee, Lord, to give,
  To one who cannot buy.

4 Empty send me not away,
  For I am come from far;
Do not, dearest Lord, delay,
  And leave me to despair;
Give me of thy flesh to eat,
  O! let me of thy nature share;
At thy banquet take my seat,
  And feast for ever there.

HYMN CCLXXXI. 7 & 6. The Coll.   J.

True experience.

1 MY LORD, how great's the favour
  That I a sinner poor,

Can

Can thro' thy blood's sweet savour
  Approach thy mercy's door,
And find an open passage
  Unto the throne of grace;
There wait the welcome message,
  That bids me; GO IN PEACE?

2 LORD, I'm an helpless creature,
   Full of the deepest need,
Throughout defil'd by nature,
   Stupid, and inly dead:
My strength is perfect weakness,
   And all I have is sin;
My heart is all uncleanness,
   A den of thieves within.

3 In this forlorn condition
   Who shall afford me aid?
Where shall I find compassion,
   But in the church's head?
JESUS, thou art all pity,
   O take me to thine arms,
And exercise thy mercy,
   To save me from all harms.

4 I'll never cease repeating
   My numberless complaints;

But

But ever be intreating
    The glorious King of saints,
Till I attain the image
    Of him I only love;
And pay my grateful homage
    With all the saints above.

5 Then I, with all in glory,
    Will thankfully relate
Th' amazing, pleasing story
    Of JESUS' love so great;
In this blest contemplation
    I ever shall be well;
And prove such consolation,
    As none below can tell.

HYMN CCLXXXII. 7 & 6, 7 & 6, three 7 & 6,
    The Coll.   J.

The Pilgrim's Song.

RISE, my soul, and stretch thy wings
    Thy better portion trace;
Rise from transitory things,
    Tow'rds heaven, thy native place:
Sun, and moon, and stars decay,
    Time shall soon this earth remove;

Rise,

Rise, my soul, and haste away
    To seats prepar'd above.

2 Rivers to the ocean run,
    Nor stay in all their course;
Fire ascending seeks the sun,
    Both speed them to their source:
So a soul that's born of GOD
    Pants to view his glorious face,
Upward tends to his abode,
    To rest in his embrace.

3 Cease, ye pilgrims, cease to mourn,
    Press onward to the prize;
Soon our Saviour will return,
    Triumphant in the skies:
Yet a season, and you know
    Happy entrance will be giv'n,
All our sorrows left below,
    And earth exchang'd for heav'n.

HYMN CCLXXXIII. Sevens. The Coll. *J.*
A prayer.

1 LORD, we come before thee now,
    At thy feet we humbly bow;
O! do not our suit disdain,
Shall we seek thee, LORD, in vain?

The VOICE of CHRIST.

2 Lord, on thee our souls depend,
In compassion now descend:
Fill our hearts with thy rich grace,
Tune our lips to sing thy praise.

3 In thine own appointed way,
Now we seek thee, here we stay;
Lord, we know not how to go,
Till a blessing thou bestow.

4 Send some message from thy word,
That may joy and peace afford;
Let thy Spirit now impart
Full salvation to each heart.

5 Comfort those who weep and mourn,
Let the time of joy return;
Those that are cast down, lift up;
Make them strong in faith and hope!

5 Grant that all may seek, and find
Thee a gracious God and kind;
Heal the sick, the captive free:
Let us all rejoice in thee!

HYMN CCLXXXIV. Sevens. The Coll. J.

The voice of Christ.

HARK! my soul, it is the Lord,
'Tis thy Saviour, hear his word;
Jesus

  Jesus speaks, and speaks to thee,
  Say, poor sinner, lov'st thou me.

2 I deliver'd thee, when bound,
  And when wounded, heal'd thy wound,
  Sought thee wand'ring, set thee right,
  Turn'd thy darkness into light.

3 Can a woman's tender care
  Cease towards the child she bare?
  Yes, she may forgetful be,
  Yet will I remember thee.

4 Mine is an unchanging love,
  Higher than the hights above,
  Deeper than the depths beneath,
  Free and faithful, strong as death.

5 Thou shall see my glory soon,
  When the work of grace is done,
  Partner of my throne shalt be,
  Say, poor sinner, lov'st thou me?

6 Lord, it is my chief complaint,
  That my love is weak and faint;
  Yet I love thee, and adore,
  O for grace to love thee more!

HYMN

DOUBTING.

HYMN CCLXXXV. Sevens. Newton. A.

Doubting.

1 'TIS a point I long to know,
    Oft it causes anxious thought;
Do I love the LORD, or no?
    Am I his, or am I not?

2 If I love, why am I thus?
    Why this dull and lifeless frame?
Hardly, sure, can they be worse
    Who have never heard his name.

Could my heart so hard remain,
    Prayer a task and burden prove,
Every trifle give me pain,
    If I knew a Saviour's love!

4 When I turn my eyes within,
    All is dark, and vain, and wild;
Fill'd with unbelief and sin,
    Can I deem myself a child?

5 If I pray, or hear, or read,
    Sin is mix'd with all I do;
You that love the LORD indeed,
    Tell me, is it thus with you?

6 Yet I mourn my stubborn will,
    Find my sin a grief and thrall;

Should

BIRTH of CHRIST.

    Should I grieve for what I feel,
        If I did not love at all?

7 Could I joy his saints to meet,
      Choose the ways I once abhor'd;
  Find, at times, the promise sweet,
      If I did not love the LORD?

8 LORD, decide the doubtful case?
      Thou, who art thy people's sun;
  Shine upon thy work of grace,
      If it be indeed begun.

9 Let me love thee more and more,
      If I love at all, I pray;
  If I have not lov'd before,
      Help me to begin To-day.

HYMN CCLXXXVI. Sevens. The Coll.   *A.*
Birth of Christ.

1 WHat good news the angels bring
    What glad tidings of our King
CHRIST our LORD is born to-day,
CHRIST who takes our sins away.
Him, who rules in heav'n and earth,
Hath in Bethleh'm his birth:
Him shall all the people see,
And rejoice eternally.

2 Lift your hearts and voices high,
　With Hosannas fill the sky;
　" Glory be to GOD above,"
　GOD is infinite in love:
　" Peace on earth, good will to men!"
　Now with us our GOD is seen:
　Angels join with us in praise!
　Help to sing redeeming grace.

3 Now the wall is broken down,
　Now the Gospel is made known;
　Now the door is open wide,
　CHRIST for Jew and Gentile dy'd.
　All who feel the weight of sin,
　All who languish to be clean;
　All who for redemption groan,
　May be sav'd by faith alone.

4 JESUS is the lovely name;
　This the angel doth proclaim;
　He shall all his people save,
　They in him remission have:
　When they see themselves undone,
　They take refuge in the Son;
　They shall all be born again,
　And with him in glory reign.

Shout ye nations of the earth,
Sing the triumphs of his birth;
All the world by him is bleft,
Sound his praife from Eaft to Weft:
Jews and Gentiles jointly sing,
CHRIST our common LORD and King,
CHRIST our life, our joy, our song,
To eternity prolong!

HYMN CCLXXXVII. Sevens. Cennick.   A.

Heavenly Journey.

CHILDREN of the heavenly King,
  As ye journey fweetly fing;
Sing your Saviour's worthy praife,
Glorious in his works and ways.

Ye are travelling home to GOD,
In the way the Fathers trod;
They are happy now, and ye
Soon their happinefs fhall fee.

O, ye banifh'd feed, be glad!
CHRIST our advocate is made;
Us to fave our flefh affumes,
Brother to our fouls becomes.

Shout, ye little flock, and bleft,
You on JESUS' throne fhall reft;
There

CHRIST our LIFE.

There your seat is now prepar'd,
There your kingdom and reward.

5 Fear not, Brethren, joyful stand,
On the borders of your land;
Jesus Christ your Father's Son
Bids you undismay'd go on.

HYMN CCLXXXVIII. Sevens. Rippon's Coll. A.

Christ our Life.

1 GRACIOUS Lord incline thine ear,
My requests vouchsafe to hear;
Hear my never ceasing cry,
Give me Christ, or else I die.

2 Lord, deny me what thou wilt,
Only ease me of my guilt;
Suppliant at thy feet I lie,
Give me Christ, or else I die.

3 All unholy and unclean,
I am nothing else but sin;
On thy mercy I rely,
Give me Christ, or else I die.

4 Thou dost freely save the lost,
In thy grace alone I trust;
With my earnest suit comply,
Give me Christ, or else I die.

5 Thou

5 Thou dost promise to forgive,
All who in thy Son believe;
LORD, I know thou canst not lie,
Give me CHRIST, or else I die.

HYMN CCLXXXIX. Sevens. The Coll. J.
Redeeming Love.

1 NOW begin the heav'nly theme,
Sing aloud in JESUS' name;
Ye, who JESUS' kindness prove,
Triumph in redeeming love.

2 Ye, who see the Father's grace,
Beaming in the Saviour's face;
As to Canaan on ye move,
Praise and bless redeeming love.

3 Mourning souls dry up your tears;
Banish all your guilty fears;
See your guilt and curse remove,
Cancell'd by redeeming love.

4 Ye, alas! who long have been,
Willing slaves to death and sin;
Now from bliss no longer rove,
Stop and taste redeeming love.

5 Welcome all by sin oppress'd,
Welcome all to JESUS CHRIST;

Nothing

Nothing brought him from above,
Nothing but redeeming love.

6 He subdued the infernal powers,
His tremendous foes and ours,
From their cursed empire drove,
Mighty in redeeming love.

7 Hither then your music bring,
Strike aloud each joyful string;
Mortals join the hosts above
Join to praise redeeming love.

HYMN CCXC. Sevens. The Coll. *J.*

Adoring Christ.

1 BRETHREN, let us join to bless
Jesus Christ our joy and peace;
Let our praise to him be giv'n,
High at God's right hand in Heav'n.

2 Master, see! to thee we bow,
Thou art Lord, and only thou;
Thou the blessed virgin's seed,
Glory of thy Church, and Head.

3 Thee the angels ceaseless sing,
Thee we praise our Priest and King;
Worthy is thy name of praise,
Full of glory, full of grace.

4 Thou

4 Thou hast the glad tidings brought,
Of salvation by thee wrought;
Wrought for all thy church! and we
Worship in their company.

5 We thy little flock adore,
Thee the LORD for ever more!
Ever with us shew thy love,
Till we join with those above.

HYMN CCXCI. Sevens. The Coll.   J.

For new-year's, Day.

WHILE with ceaseless course the sun
   Hasted thro' the former year,
Many souls their race have run,
   Never more to meet us here:
Fix'd in an eternal state,
   They have done with all below;
We a little longer wait,
   But how little, none can know

2 As the winged arrow flies
   Speedily the mark to find,
As the light'ning from the skies
   Darts, and leaves no trace behind;
Swiftly thus our fleeting days
   Bear us down life's rapid stream;

Upwards,

  Upwards, LORD, our spirits raise;
   All below is but a dream.

3 Thanks for mercies past receive;
  Pardon of our sins renew;
 Teach us henceforth how to live
  With eternity in view.
 Bless the word to young and old,
  Fill us with a Saviour's love;
 And when life's short tale is told,
  May we dwell with thee above.

HYMN CCXCII. Sevens, with Hall. The Coll. *J.*

Praising God.

GLORY be to GOD on high, Hallelujah
 GOD, whose glory fills the sky;
Peace on earth to man forgiv'n,
Man, the well-belov'd of heav'n.

2 Sov'reign Father, heav'nly King, Hall.
 Thee we now presume to sing;
 Glad thine attributes confess,
 Glorious all, and numberless.

3 Hail, by all thy works ador'd,
 Hail the everlasting LORD;
 Thee, with thankful hearts we prove,
 LORD of pow'r, and GOD of love!

HYMN

HYMN CCXCIII. 8 twice six. The Coll. J.

Morning.

1 RISE my soul adore thy maker;
   Angels praise join thy lays,
 With them be partaker.

2 Sov'reign LORD of ev'ry spirit,
   In thy light lead me right,,
 Thro' my Saviour's merit.

3 Thou this night waft my protector,
   With me stay all this day,
 Ever my director.

4 Leave me not, but ever love me;
   Let thy peace be my bliss,
 Till thou hence remove me.

5 Holy, holy, holy giver,
   Of all good, life and food,
 Reign ador'd for ever.

6 Glory, honour, thanks, and blessing,
   One in three, give we thee,
 Never, never ceasing.

HYMN CCXCIV. 8 & 2 6. The Coll. J.

Evening.

1 ERE I sleep for ev'ry favour,
   This day shew'd and bestow'd,
           I will

I will bless my Saviour.

2 O my LORD! what shall I render
 To thy name, still the same,
Gracious, good and tender.

3 Leave me not, but ever love me;
 Let thy peace be my bliss,
Till thou hence remove me.

4 Visit me with thy salvation;
 Let thy care now be near,
Round my habitation.

5 Thou my rock, my guard, my tow'r,
 Safely keep, while I sleep,
Me, with all thy pow'r.

6 And, whene'er in death I slumber,
 Let me rise with the wise,
Counted in their number.

HYMN CCXCV. 2 of 8, and 1 of 6 & dotts.

Finished Redemption.   The Coll.   *A.*

1 'TIS finished the Redeemer said,
 And meekly bow'd his dying head,
Whilst we this sentence scan,
Come sinners, and observe the word,
Behold the conquest of the LORD
Complete for helpless man.

2 Finish'd

2 Finish'd the righteousness of grace,
  Finish'd for sinners pard'ning peace;
    Their mighty debt is paid:
  Accusing law cancell'd by blood,
  And wrath of an offended God
    In sweet oblivion laid.

3 Who now shall urge a second claim?
  The law no longer can condemn;
    Faith a release can shew;
  Justice itself a friend appears,
  The prison house a whisper hears,
    " Loose him and let him go."

4 O unbelief! injurious bar!
  Source of tormenting, fruitless fear
    Why dost thou yet reply?
  Where'er thy loud objections fall,
  " 'Tis finish'd," still may answer all
    And silence ev'ry cry.

HYMN CCXCVI. Twice 8 & 6. The Coll. *J.*

Spiritual Barrenness.

1 Most righteous God my doom I bear
  My load of guilt my pain and care
    Inflam'd to base desires;
  Hard toiling for embitter'd bread,

I mourn

    I mourn my barren soul o'erspread,
      With cursed thorns and briars.

2 Death's sentence in myself receive,
   And dust to dust already cleave,
     Exil'd from paradise;
   Hast'ning to hellish misery,
   Jesus, if unredeem'd by thee,
     My soul forever dies.

3 But Jesus hath my sentence born,
   He did in my affliction mourn;
     A man of sorrow made;
   A servant and a curse for me,
   He bore the utmost penalty,
     He suffer'd in my stead.

4 I see him sweat great drops of blood,
   I see him faint beneath my load,
     The thorns his temples tear;
   He bows his bleeding head and dies!
   He lives! he mounts above the skies!
     He claims my Eden there!

HYMN CCXCVII. Twice 8 & 6. The Coll. J.
For Seriousness.

1 THOU God of glorious majesty!
    To thee, against myself, to thee,

   A worm of earth I cry:
An half-awaken'd child of man,
An heir of endless bliss or pain,
   A sinner born to die.

Lo! on a narrow neck of land,
'Twixt two unbounded seas I stand,
   Secure, insensible!
A point of time, a moment's space,
Removes me to the heav'nly place,
   Or shuts me up in hell.

O God, mine inmost soul convert!
And deeply on my thoughtful heart
   Eternal things impress;
Give me to feel their solemn weight,
And tremble on the brink of fate,
   And 'wake to righteousness.

Before me place in dread array,
The pomp of that tremendous day,
   When thou with clouds shalt come,
To judge the nations at thy bar,
And tell me, Lord, shall I be there,
   To meet a joyful doom!

Be this my great one business here.
With serious industry and fear,

My future bliſs t'inſure;
Thine utmoſt counſel to fulfill,
And ſuffer all thy righteous will,
And to the end endure.

6 Then, Saviour, then my ſoul receive,
Tranſported from this vale to live,
And reign with thee above;
Where faith is ſweetly loſt in ſight,
And hope in full ſupreme delight,
And everlaſting love.

HYMN CCXCVII. twice 8 & 6. The Coll. *J.*

The ſinner converted.

WHEN with my mind divinely preſt
Dear Saviour, my revolving breaſt
Wou'd paſt offences trace;
Trembling I make the black review,
Yet pleas'd behold admiring too,
The pow'r of changing grace.

2 This tongue with blaſphemies defil'd,
Theſe feet, to erring paths beguil'd,
In heav'nly league agree;
Who cou'd believe ſuch lips cou'd praiſe
Or think my dark and winding ways
Should ever lead to thee?

3 Theſe

3 These eyes that once abus'd their sight,
 Now lift to thee their wat'ry light,
  And weep a silent flood;
 These hands ascend in ceaseless pray'r;
 O wash away the stains they wear,
  In pure redeeming blood!

4 These ears, that pleas'd cou'd entertain
 The midnight oath, the lustful strain,
  When round the festal board;
 Now deaf to all th' inchanting noise,
 Avoid the throng, detest the joys,
  And press to hear thy word.

5 Thus art thou serv'd in ev'ry part;
 And now thou dost transform my heart,
  That drossy thing refine:
 Now grace doth nature's strength controul
 And a new creature---body---soul,
  Are, LORD, for ever thine!

HYMN CCXCVIII. P. M. twice 8 & 6 & three 8
 & 6. Lyric Poems. 4.
Converse with Christ.

I'M tir'd with visits, modes and forms,
 And flatteries paid to fellow worms
  Their conversation cloys:

Their vain amours, and empty stuff:
But I can ne'er enjoy enough
Of thy blest company, my LORD, thou
life of all my joys.

2 When he begins to tell his love,
Through every vein my passions move,
The captives of his tongue;
In midnight shades, on frosty ground,
I could attend the pleasing sound,
Nor should I feel *December* cold, nor
think the darkness long.

3 There while I hear my Saviour GOD
Count o'er the sins (a heavy load)
He bore upon the tree,
Inward I blush with secret shame,
And weep, and love, and bless the name
That knew not guilt nor grief his own,
but bare it all for me.

4 Next he describes the thorns he wore,
And talks his bloody passion o'er,
Till I am drown'd in tears:
Yet with the sympathetic smart
There's a strange joy beats round my heart
The cursed tree has blessings in't, my
sweetest balm it bears.

5 I hear the glorious sufferer tell,
   How on his cross he vanquish'd hell,
      And all the pow'rs beneath:
   Transported and inspir'd, my tongue
   Attempts his triumphs in a song:
How has the serpent lost his sting, and
      where's thy victory, death?

6 But when he shews his hands and heart
   With those dear prints of dying smart
      He sets my soul on fire:
   Not the beloved John could rest
   With more delight upon that breast,
Nor Thomas pry into those wounds with
      more intense desire.

7 Kindly he opens me his ear,
   And bids me pour my sorrows there,
      And tell him all my pains:
   Thus while I ease my burden'd heart,
   In ev'ry woe he bears a part,
His arms embrace me, and his hand my
      drooping head sustains.

8 Fly from my thoughts, all human things
   And sporting swains, and fighting kings,
      And tales of wanton love;

My soul disdains that little snare
The tangles of Amira's hair;
Thine arms, my God, are sweeter bands,
nor can my heart remove.

HYMN CCXCIX. 8 & 7. The Coll. *J.*

Isaiah ix, 2.

LIGHT of those whose dreary dwelling
Borders on the shades beneath,
Come and by thy love's revealing,
Dissipate the clouds beneath:
The new heav'n and earth's Creator,
In our deepest darkness rise!
Scatt'ring all the night of nature,
Pouring eye-sight on our eyes!

2 Still we wait for thine appearing,
Life and joy thy beams impart;
Chasing all our fears, and chearing
Ev'ry poor benighted heart:
Come, and manifest the favour
God has for our ransom'd race;
Come, thou All sufficient Saviour,
Come and bring thy gospel-grace.

3 Save us in thy great compassion,
O thou mild pacific Prince!

Give

Give the knowledge of salvation,
   Give the pardon of our sins!
By thine all-restoring merit,
   Ev'ry burden'd soul release;
Ev'ry weary, wand'ring spirit,
   Guide into thy perfect peace.

HYMN CCC. twice 8 & 7.   The Coll.   J.
          To Jesus Christ.

HAIL, thou once despised Jesus!
   Hail, thou Galilean King!
Who didst suffer to release us,
   Who didst free salvation bring!
Hail, thou agonizing Saviour,
   Who hast borne our sin and shame;
By whose merits we find favour,
   Life is given thro' thy name!

Paschal Lamb by God appointed,
   All our sins were on thee laid!
By Almighty love anointed,
   Thou hast full atonement made;
Ev'ry sin may be forgiv'n,
   Thro' the virtue of thy blood;
Open'd is the gate of Heav'n
   Peace is made 'twixt man and God.

I 4   3 Jesus,

3 JESUS, hail! enthron'd in glory,
  There for ever to abide!
All the heav'nly hosts adore thee,
  Seated at thy Father's side:
There for sinners thou art pleading,
  Spare them yet another year.---
Thou for saints art interceeding,
  Till in glory they appear.

4 Worship, honour, pow'r and blessing,
  CHRIST is worthy to receive---
Loudest praises without ceasing,
  Meet it is for us to give!
Help, ye bright angelic spirits,
  Bring your sweetest, noblest lays,
Help to sing our Saviour's merits,
  Help to chaunt IMMANUEL's praise.

HYMN CCCI Eight and Seven   The Coll.   J.
Christ the believer's All.

1 Lamb of God we fall before thee
    Humbly trusting in thy cross;
  That alone be all our glory,
    All things else are dung and dross;
  Thee we own a perfect Saviour,
    Only source of all that's good:

Ev'ry

CHRIST THE BELIEVER'S ALL.

Ev'ry grace and ev'ry favour
    Come to us thro' Jesus' blood.

Jesus gives us true repentance,
    By his Spirit sent from Heav'n;
Jesus whispers this sweet sentence,
    "Son thy sins are all forgiv'n;"
Faith he gives us to believe it,
    Grateful hearts his love to prize;
Want we wisdom he must give it;
    Hearing ears and seeing eyes.

Jesus gives us pure affections,
    Wills to do what he requires;
Makes us follow his directions,
    And, what he commands, inspires;
All our pray'rs and all our praises,
    Rightly offer'd in his name;
He that dictates them is Jesus;
    He that answers is the same.

When we live on Jesus' merit,
    Then we worship God aright:
Father, Son and Holy Spirit,
    Then we savingly unite,
This the whole conclusion of it,

Great or good whate'er we call;
God, or King or Prieſt, or Prophet,
Jeſus Chriſt is, all in all.

HYMN CCCII Eight and Seven   Rippon's Coll.   J.

Buried with Chriſt in Baptiſm.   Rom. vi, 4.

1 JESUS, mighty King in Sion!
    Thou alone our guide ſhalt be;
Thy commiſſion we rely on,
    We would follow none but thee.

2 As an emblem of thy paſſion,
    And thy vict'ry o'er the grave,
We, who know thy great ſalvation,
    Are baptiz'd beneath the wave.

3 Fearleſs of the world's deſpiſing,
    We the ancient path purſue,
Buried with our Lord, and riſing
    To a life divinely new.

HYMN CCCIII Eight and Seven   The Coll.   J.

An happy moment.

1 SAviour, I do feel thy merit,
    Sprinkled with redeeming blood,
And my weary troubled ſpirit,
    Now finds reſt in thee, my God:
I am ſafe, and I am happy,

While

HAPPY MOMENT.

> While in thy dear arms I lie!
> Sin and satan cannot hurt me,
> While the Saviour is so nigh.

2 Now I'll sing of Jesus' merit,
  Tell the world of his dear name,
That if any want his Spirit,
  He is still the very same:
He that asketh soon receiveth,
  He that seeks is sure to find;
Come, for whosoe'er believeth,
  He will never cast behind.

3 Now our advocate is pleading,
  With his Father and our God;
Now for us he's interceeding,
  As the purchase of his blood:
Now me thinks I hear him pleading,
  "Father save them I have dy'd;"
And the Father, answers, saying,
  "They are freely justify'd."

HYMN CCCIV Eight and Seven. Robison. J.
1 Sam. vii, 12.

1 Come thou font of ev'ry blessing!
    Tune my heart to sing thy grace!
  Streams of mercy never-ceasing,

Call for songs of loudest praise:
Teach me some melodious sonnet,
Sung by flaming tongues above;
Praise the mount---I'm fixt upon it,
Mount of God's unchanging love.

2 Here I raise my Eben-Ezer,
Hither by thy help I'm come;
And I hope by thy good pleasure
Safely to arrive at home.
Jesus sought me when a stranger,
Wand'ring from the fold of God;
He to rescue me from danger,
Interpos'd with precious blood.

3 O! to grace how great a debtor
Daily I'm constrain'd to be!
Let that grace, Lord like a fetter,
Bind my wand'ring heart to thee!

Prone to wander, Lord, I feel it;
Prone to leave the God I love---
Here's my heart, Lord, take and seal it;
Seal it from thy courts above!

HYMN CCCV Eight and Seven The Coll.

1 COME, descend, O heav'nly Spirit,
Fan, each spark into a flame;

Blessing

O HEAVENLY SPIRIT.

Blessings let us now inherit,
   Blessings that we cannot name:
Whilst Hosannas we are singing,
   May our hearts in rapture move,
Feel new grace in them still springing,
   Breathe the air of purest love.

Let us sail in grace's ocean,
   Float on that unbounded sea,
Guided into pure devotion,
   Kept from paths of error free:
On thy heav'nly manna feeding,
   Skreen'd from ev'ry envious foe;
Love, O love for sinners bleeding,
   All for thee we would forego.

Keep us, Lord, still in communion,
   Daily nearer drawn to thee;
Singing in the sweetest union
   Of that heart-felt mystery:
Keep us safe from each delusion,
   Well protected from all harm;
Free from sin and all confusion,
   Circle us within thine arms.

DEATH AND GLORY.

HYMN CCCVI. Eight and Seven. The Coll. *J.*
Death and Glory.

1 IN a world of sin and sorrow,
 Compass'd round with many a care
From eternity we borrow
 Hope, that can exclude despair:
Thee triumphant God and Saviour!
 In the glass of faith we see;
O assist each faint endeavour!
 Raise our earth-born souls to thee.

2 Place that awful scene before us,
 Of the last tremendous day;
When to life thou shalt restore us,
 Ling'ring ages, haste away!
Then this vile and sinful nature
 In corruption shall put on;
Life renewing, glorious Saviour!
 Let thy gracious will be done.

HYMN CCCVII. 8 & 7 The Coll. *J.*
The Resurrection of Christ.

1 PLEAS'D we read in sacred story,
 How our Lord resum'd his breath;
Where, O grave's, thy conqu'ring glory
 Where's thy sting, thou fantom death?
Soon thy jaws, restrain'd from chewing,

  Must disgorge their ransom'd prey:
Man first gave thee pow'r to ruin,
  Man too takes that pow'r away.

2 I am Alpha, says the Saviour;
  I Omega likewise am;
I was dead and live forever,
  God Almighty and th' Lamb,
In the Lord is our perfection,
  And in him our boast we'll make;
We shall share his resurrection,
  If we of his death partake.

3 Ye that die without repentance,
  Ye must rise when Christ appears;
Rise to hear your dreadful sentence,
  While the saints rejoice in theirs:
You to dwell with fiends infernal,
  They with Jesus Christ to reign:
They go into life eternal,
  You to everlasting pain.

5 Bold rebellion, base backsliding,
  Stop your course, reflect with dread;
In destruction there's no hiding;
  Death and hell give up their dead,
Ev'ry sea, and lake, and river

JUDGMENT.

Shall restore their dead to view:
Shout for gladness, O believer
Christ is ris'n, and so shall you.

HYMN CCCVIII.   8 & 7, twice 7.   A
Judgment.

1 PRess'd my soul with future prospect,
   Sing creation's dismal end;
Long foretold by sacred Prophets,
Holy Muse thy succours lend.
Say what horror what confusion,
Will each sinful heart dismay;
What distresses, tortures, anguish,
Reign in that tremendous day.

2 Rumbling Thunders forky lightnings,
Ghastly glaring thwart the gloom;
Nature shaking to her center,
Groans prophetic of her doom.
Cliffy rocks and lofty mountains,
O'er the trembling basis rock;
While Earth yawns in dreaful chasme,
With each strong repeated shock.

3 Seas with horrid palpitation,
Ravage round their frighted shores,
Blustering wind with frantic fury,
Through each ruin'd fabric roars,
The Sun's bright orb is veil'd in sackcloth
                              Stripp'd

JUDGMENT. 305

Stripp'd of all his sparkling beams;
The moon has dropp'd her silver radiance
And diffolves in purple ftreams.

4 Stars of light divinely brilliant,
Studding night, Cimmerian robe;
Hurl'd in darknefs from their orbits,
Each a darken'd ruin'd globe.
Hark! the martial trumpet founding
Rends in twain the cryftal fky;
Vengeance blazing lights the concave
Of profound eternity.

5 See the fovereign Æther furling;
Nobler fcenes falutes mine eyes;
Heav'n in folemn pomp defcending,
Crimfon banners drefs the fkies.
On the arched ftriped rainbow,
Sits enthron'd the eternal God,
Myriads of Celeftial Warriors.
Round him wait his awful nod.

6 Go, he cries, ye winged herald,
Bring my faints from ev'ry wind, [fom'd
Thofe my blood from death has ran-
Thofe in life's fair volume penn'd,
Strait a holy troop obfequious,
Swift as lightning fkim'd along,

And

And from ev'ry grave collecting,
Jesus' dear redeemed Throng.

7 Death no more with livid aspect,
Spurs his fallow steed to stay;
Now the ravenous foe disgorges,
All his long imprison'd prey,
Rous'd from Tombs each wicked rises,
By the trumpet's thrilling sound,
Round they stare with wild amazement,
Wond'ring at the scene profound.

8 Fill'd with horror dread and anguish,
Rocks and mountains they implore,
To fall and crush them out of being;
Wishing now to be no more.
Hark the Herald calls to judgment,
Justice draws her glittering sword,
Lightning glances from his aspect;
Thunder clothes his awful word.

9 Go ye cursed fill'd with vengeance,
Nor for peace my name invoke;
Ye who once despis'd my mercy,
And my fury dare provoke:
Go to pits of burning sulphur,

Ever banish'd from my rest,
Where the souls eternal larum,
Ceaseless beats your pulsive breast.

HYMN CCCIX. 8 and 7, Newport Coll. A.
Judgment.

LO, th' Almighty King of Glory,
 Sends his awful summons forth!
Calls the nations all before him!
 From the east, south, west and north!
His loud trumpet, his loud trumpet, his
 loud trumpet,
 Rends the tombs the dead awake!

Now behold the dead arising;
 Great and small before him stand;
Not one soul forgot, or missing,
 None his orders countermand;
All stand waiting, all stand waiting all
 stand waiting,
 For their last decisive doom.

Now the Saviour; once despised,
 Comes to judge the quick and dead:
See his foes each one with horror,
 Lifting up his guilty head.
How they tremble; how they tremble,

how

JUDGMENT.

how they tremble!
At the Lamb's tremendous bar!

4 Now they see him on the rainbow,
   With his countless guards around;
Saints and Angels his retinue,
   With their harps of sweetest sound.
Hallelujah! Hallelujah! Hallelujah;
   Echoes sweet from all the choir.

5 Now his chosen gladly meet him,
   All seraphic all divine!
Lo, they join the glorious army,
   Whose bright robes the sun outshine!
All triumphant! all triumphant! all triumphant,
   See the grand Redeemed throng.

6 Then behold the dreadful sentence,
   On the foes of Christ is past:
Down to hell without repentance,
   All the guilty croud is cast,
While the ransom'd, while the ransom'd, while the ransom'd,
   All applaud the righteous doom,

7 Now attend the noble army,
   Wash'd in their Redeemer's blood;

Swift

Swift and joyful is their journey,
  To the palace of their God!
All victorious! all victorious! all victorious,
  Hallelujah to the lamb!
    Epiphonema,
O ye sinners now give glory,
  To the great eternal Three!
While such danger lies before you,
  Can you unconcerned be?
Judgment hastens! Judgment hastens!
    Judgment hastens:
Mercy, mercy now implore!

HYMN CCCX. The Coll. *A.*
Judgment.

1 LO he comes in clouds descending,
    Once for helpless sinners slain!
  Thousand, thousand saints attending,
  Swell the triumph of his train.
    Hallelujah, Hallelujah, Hallelujah,
    All the Angels cry amen.

2 Ev'ry eye shall now behold him,
    Rob'd in dreadful majesty,
  Those who set at nought and sold him,

Pierc'd

JUDGMENT.

Pierc'd and nail'd him to the tree.
 Deeply wailing, &c.
 Shall the true Messiah see.

3 Ev'ry island, sea, and mountain,
  Heav'n and earth, shall flee away;
 All who hate him, must confounded,
  Hear the trump proclaim the day;
   Come to judgment, &c.
   Come to judgment come away.

4 Now redemption long expected,
  See, in solemn pomp appear!
 All his saints by man rejected,
  Now shall meet him in the air!
   Hallelujah, &c.
   See the day of God appear.

5 Answer thine own bride and Spirit,
  Hasten Lord the gen'ral doom,
 The new heav'n and earth t'inherit,
  Take thy pining exiles home,
   All creation, &c.
   Travails! groans! and bids thee come.

6 Yea, amen let all adore thee,
  High on thy eternal throne!

Saviour,

Saviour, take the pow'r and glory;
  Claim the kingdom for thine own,
O come quickly, &c.
  Hallelujah! come Lord come.

HYMN CCCXI. The Coll.

Judgment.

LO! he cometh, countless trumpets,
  Blow before the bloody sign;
'Midst ten thousand saints and angels,
  See the crucified shine.
Hallelujah! Hallelujah! Hallelujah!
Welcome welcome bleeding lamb!

2 Now his merit by the harpers,
  Thro' th' eternal deep resounds;
Now resplendent shine his nail-prints,
  Ev'ry eye shall see his wounds,
They who pierc'd him, &c. &c.
  Shall at his appearance wail.

Ev'ry island, sea, and mountain,
  Heav'n and earth shall flee away,
All who hate him, must ashamed,
  Hear the trump proclaim the day:
Come to judgment, &c. &c.
  Stand before the son of man.

4 Saints

JUDGMENT.

4 Saints who love him, view his glory,
    Shining in his bruised face,
His dear person on the rainbow,
    Now his people's head shall raise:
      Happy mourners, &c. &c.
Lo! in clouds, he comes, he comes!

5 Now redemption, long expected,
    See! in solemn pomp appear;
All his people once rejected,
    Now shall meet him in the air:
      Hallelujah! &c. &c.
Now the promis'd kingdom's come.

6 View him smiling now determin'd
    Ev'ry evil to destroy;
All the nations now shall sing him,
    Songs of everlasting joy:
      O come quickly, &c. &c.
Hallelujah come Lord come.

HYMN CCCXII. 8 and 7 Altered by Toplady.   *J.*

(Helmsley tune.)   *Invitation.*

1 Come ye sinners poor and wretched,
    Weak and wounded, sick and sore
Jesus ready stands to save you,
    Full of pity, love and pow'r;
      He is able

INVITATION.

He is willing; doubt no more.
Ho! ye needy, come and welcome,
   God's free bounty glorify
True belief and true repentance,
   Every grace that brings us nigh
     Without money
Come to Jesus Christ and buy.

Let not conscience make you linger
   Nor of fitness fondly dream;
All the fitness he requireth
   Is to feel your need of him
     This he gives you,
'Tis the Spirit's glimm'ring beam.

Agonizing in the garden,
   Lo your Maker prostrate lies!
On the bloody tree behold him,
   Hear him cry before he dies,
     It is finish'd"
Sinner will not this suffice?

Lo! th' incarnate God ascended,
   Pleads the merit of his blood,
Venture on him, venture freely
   Let no other trust intrude,
     None but Jesus

DISMISSION.

Can do helpless sinners good.

6 Saints and angels join'd in concert
   Sing the praises of the Lamb,
While the blissfull seats of Heaven
   Sweetly echo with his name.
     Hallelujah!
Sinners here may do the same.

HYMN CCCXIII 8 & 7, 8 & 7, 4 & 7, Rippon's Coll. J.

Dismission.

1 LORD dismiss us with a blessing,
   Fill our hearts with joy and peace,
Let us each thy love possessing,
   Triumph in redeeming grace:
     O refresh us!
Trav'ling through this wilderness.

2 Thanks we give and adoration,
   For thy gospel's joyful sound,
May the fruit of thy salvation,
   In our hearts and lives abound:
     May thy presence,
With us ever more be found.

3 So whene'er the signal's given,
   Us from earth to call away,
Borne on Angels wings to Heaven,

                  Glad

FINISHED REDEMPTION.

Glad to leave our cumb'rous clay,
   May we ready,
Rise and reign in endless day.

HYMN CCCXIV. twice 8 & 7, 4 & 7, Rippon's Coll. J.
Finished Redemption.

Hark! the voice of love and mercy,
   Sounds aloud from Calvary!
See it rends the rocks asunder,
   Shakes the earth and veil's the sky!
      "It is finish'd!"
Hear the dying Saviour cry!

It is finish'd! O what pleasure
   Do these charming words afford!
Heavenly blessings without measure,
   Flow to us from Christ the Lord.
      It is finish'd!
Saints, the dying words record.

Finish'd all the types and shadows
   Of the ceremonial law!
Finish'd all that God hath promis'd:
   Death and hell no more shall awe.
      It is finish'd
Saints, from hence your comfort draw.

INVITATION.

4 Tune your harps anew, ye seraphs,
   Join to sing the pleasing theme:
All on earth and all in heaven,
   Join to praise Immanuel's name!
   Hallelujah!
Glory to the bleeding Lamb.

HYMN CCCXV.   The Coll.   *J.*
Invitation.

1 COME, ye sinners, come to Jesus,
   Think upon your gracious Lord;
He has pity'd your condition,
   He has sent his gospel word.
   Mercy calls you,
Mercy flows on Jesus' blood.

2 Dearest Saviour help thy servant
   To proclaim thy wond'rous love:
Pour thy grace upon this people,
   That thy truth they may approve;
   Bless O bless them
From thy shining courts above.

3 Now thy gracious word invites them
   To partake the gospel-feast:
Let thy Spirit sweetly draw them,
   Ev'ry soul be Jesus' guest.

FOR REVIVAL.

O receive us
Let us find thy promis'd rest.

HYMN CCCXVI. 8 & 7, 8 & 7, 4 & 8, or 12 & 7.
Alter'd by Ryland. J.
Prayer for Revival.

SAVIOUR visit thy plantation,
  Grant us LORD a gracious rain!
All will come to desolation,
  Unless thou return again:
LORD, revive us,
All our help must come from thee.

Keep no longer at a distance,
  Shine upon us from on high;
Lest for want of thine assistance,
  Ev'ry plant should droop and die.
   Lord, &c.

Surely, once thy garden flourish'd,
  Ev'ry part look'd gay and green;
Then thy word our spirits nourish'd,
  Happy seasons we have seen! Lord &c.

But a drought has since succeeded,
  And a sad decline we see;
LORD, thy help is greatly needed,
Help can only come from thee. Lord &c.

5 Where

5 Where are those we counted leaders,
    Fill'd with zeal, and love, and truth
Old professors, tall as cedars,
    Bright examples to our youth. Lord &c

6 Some in whom we once delighted,
    We shall meet no more below,
Some, alas! we fear are blighted,
    Scarce a single leaf they show. Lord &c

7 Younger plants---the sight how pleasan
    Cover'd thick with blossoms stood;
But they cause us grief at present,
    Frosts have nipp'd them in the bud!
    Lord, &c.

8 Dearest Saviour, hasten hither,
    Thou canst make them bloom again
Oh, permit them not to wither,
    Let not all our hopes be vain; Lord, &c

9 Let our mutual love be fervent,
    Make us prevalent in prayers;
Let each one esteem'd thy servant,
    Shun the world's bewitching snares:
    Lord, &c.

10 Break the tempter's fatal power,
   Turn the stony heart to flesh;
And begin, from this good hour,
   To revive thy work afresh:
Lord, revive us,
   All our help must come from thee.

HYMN CCCXVII. 8 & 7, 8 & 7, twice 7. The Coll. J.
The word of God more precious than gold.

1 PRECIOUS Bible! what a treasure
   Does the word of God afford?
All I want for life and pleasure,
   Food and medicine, shield and sword:
Let the world account me poor,
Having this I want no more.

2 Food to which the world's a stranger,
   Here my hungry soul enjoys;
Of excess there is no danger,
   Tho' it fills, it never cloys.
On a dying Christ I feed,
Here is meat and drink indeed.

3 When my faith is faint and sickly,
   Or when satan wounds my mind,
Cordials to revive me quickly,
   Healing medicines here I find:

To the promises I flee,
Each affords a remedy.

4 In the hour of dark temptation,
   Satan cannot make me yield;
For the word of consolation
   Is to me a mighty shield.
While the scripture-truths endure,
From his pow'r I am secure.

HYMN CCCXVIII. 8 & 7, 8 & 7, twice 7:
The Coll.   A.
Praise to the Redeemer.

1 LET us love and sing and wonder,
   Let us praise the Saviour's name;
He has hush'd the law's loud thunder,
He has quench'd mount Sinai's flame;
   He has wash'd us with his blood,
   He has brought us nigh to GOD.

2 Let us sing, tho' fierce temptation
Threaten hard to bear us down;
For the LORD our strong salvation,
Holds in view the conqu'ror's crown,
   He who wash'd us with his blood,
   Soon will bring us home to GOD.

Let us wonder, grace and justice
Join and point to mercy's store:
When thro' grace in CHRIST our trust is
Justice smiles and asks no more.
    He who wash'd us with his blood,
    Has secur'd our way to GOD.

Let us praise and join the chorus
Of the saints enthron'd on high!
Here they trusted him before us,
Now their praises fill the sky,
    Thou hast wash'd us with thy blood,
    Thou art worthy, Lamb of GOD!

Yes we praise thee, glorious Saviour;
Wonder, love and bless thy name;
Pardon, LORD, our poor endeavour,
Pity, for thou know'st our frame.
    Wash our souls and songs with blood,
    For by thee we come to GOD.

HYMN CCCXIX. Twice 8 & 7 Do. The Coll.   J.
Relative Duties

CHristians in your several stations,
    Dutiful to all relations,
Give to each his proper due,
Let not their unkind behaviour,

                              Make

Make you disobey your Saviour,
His command's the rule for you.

2 Parents be to children tender,
Children, full obedience render,
  To your parents in the Lord;
Never slight nor disrespect them,
Nor thro' pride, when old reject them;
  'Tis the precept of the word.

3 Wives, to Husbands yield subjection;
Husband with a kind affection,
  Cherish, as yourselves, your wives,
Masters rule with moderation,
Sway'd by justice, not by passion,
  To the scriptures square your lives.

4 Servants, serve your masters truly;
Not unfaithful, nor unruly,
  To the good nor to the bad,
Not refusing what you'r bidden;
Nor replying when you'r chidden,
  'Tis the ordinance of God.

5 This shall solve th' important question,
Whether thou'rt a real Christian,
  Better than each golden dream:
Better far than lip expression,

Tow'ring

Tow'ring notions, great profession,
This shall shew your love to him.

HYMN CCCXX. Twice 8 & 7 Do. The Collection.
Isaiah, (liii)   J.

WHO hath our report believed,
    Shiloh come, is not received,
  Not received by his own;
Promis'd Branch from root of Jesse,
David's offspring sent to bless ye,
  Come too meekly to be known.

Like a tender plant that's growing
Where no water's friendly flowing,
  No kind rains refresh the ground:
Drooping, dying we shall view him,
See no charm to draw us to him,
  There no beauty will be seen

Lo! Messiah unrespected,
Man of grief, despis'd, rejected,
  Wounds his form disfig'ring,
Marr'd his visage more than any,
For he bears the sin of many,
  All our sorrows carrying.

No deceit his mouth hath spoken,
Blameless, he no law had broken;

Yet

ISAIAH, LIII.

    Yet was number'd with the worst :
  For, because the LORD wou'd grieve him
  We, who saw it, did believe him
    For his own offences curst.

5 But while him our thoughts accused,
  He for us alone was bruised,
    Stricken, smitten for our guilt:
  With his stripes our wounds are cured,
  By his pains our peace assured,
    Purchas'd by the blood he spilt.

6 Love amazing so to mind us!
  Shepherd come from heaven to find us
    Silly sheep all gone astray!
  Lost, undone by our transgressions;
  Worse than stript of all possessions,
    Debtors without hope to pay.

7 Fear our portion, slaves in spirit,---
  He redeem'd us by his merit,
    To a glorious liberty:
  Dearly first his goodness bought us,
  Truth and love then sweetly taught us;
    Truth and love have made us free.

8 Blessed be the pow'r who gave us,
  Freely gave his Son to save us;

Bless'd the Son, who freely came:
Honour, blessing, adoration,
Ever from the whole creation
Be to GOD, and to the Lamb.

HYMN CCCXXI. Five 8 & 7. The Coll.　　*J.*

Judgment.

HE comes! he comes! the judge severe
The seventh trumpet speaks him near
His lightnings flash, his thunders roll,
He's welcome to the faithful soul;
Welcome, welcome, welcome, welcome
Welcome to the faithful soul.

2 From heav'n angelic voices sound,
See th' Almighty JESUS crown'd!
Girt with omnipotence and grace,
And glory decks the Saviour's face;
Glory, glory, glory, glory,
Glory decks the Saviour's face.

3 Descending on his azure throne,
He claims the kingdoms as his own;
The kingdoms all obey his word,
And hail him their triumphant LORD;
Hail him, hail him, hail him, hail him,
Hail him their triumphant LORD.

4 Shout

4 Shout all ye people of the sky,
And all the saints of the most high:
Our GOD, who now his right obtains,
For ever, and for ever reigns,
Ever, ever, ever, ever,
Ever, and for ever reigns.

5 The Father praise, the Son adore,
The Spirit bless for evermore:
Salvation's glorious work is done,
We welcome the great three in one;
Welcome, welcome, welcome, welcome
Welcome the great three in one.

HYMN CCCXXII. Eights, of twice 3 syllables & 2

Christ withdrawn. The Coll. *J.*

1 O What shall I do to retrieve,
The love for a season bestow'd;
'Tis better to die than to live
Exil'd from the presence of GOD:
With sorrow distracted and doubt,
With palpable horror opprest,
The city I wander about,
And seek my repose in his breast.

2 Ye watchman of Israel, declare,
If ye my beloved have seen,

And point to that heav'nly fair,
　　　Surpassing the children of men:
My Lover and LORD from above,
　　Who only can quiet my pain,
Whom only I languish to love,
　　O where shall I find him again?

3　The joy and desire of mine eyes,
　　　The end of my sorrow and woe;
My hope, and my heav'nly prize,
　　My height of ambition below:
Once more if he shew me his face,
　　He never again shall depart,
Detain'd in my closest embrace,
　　Conceal'd in the depth of my heart.

HYMN CCCXXIII. Eights. New Jerusalem.
　　　Newton.　　　J.
　　What think ye of Christ? Matt. 22 xlii.

WHAT think ye of Christ; is the test
　　To try both your state & your scheme,
You cannot be right in the rest,
　　Unless you think rightly of him;
As JESUS appears in your view,
　　As he is beloved or not,
So GOD is disposed to you,
　　And mercy or wrath is your lot.

2 Some

2 Some take him a creature to be,
    A man, or an angel at moſt;
Sure theſe have not feelings like me,
    Nor know themſelves utterly loſt:
So guilty, ſo helpleſs am I,
    I durſt not confide in his blood,
Nor on his protection rely,
    Unleſs I were ſure he's a God.

3 Some call him a Saviour in word,
    But mix their own works with his plan
And hope he his help will afford,
    When they have done all that they can.
If doings prove rather too light,
    (A little they own, they may, fail)
They purpoſe to make up full weight,
    By caſting his name in the ſcale.

4 Some ſtile him the pearl of great price,
    And ſay he's the fountain of joys;
Yet feed upon folly and vice,
    And cleave to the world and its toys
Like Judas, the Saviour they kiſs,
    And as they ſalute him betray;
Ah! what will profeſſion like this,
    Avail in his terrible day.

5 If ask'd what of Jesus I think?
   Tho' still my best thoughts are but poor
 I say, he's my meat and my drink,
   My life and my strength and my store,
 My shepherd, my husband, my friend,
   My Saviour from sin & from thrall,
 My hope from beginning to end,
   My portion, my Lord, and my All.

HYMN CCCXXIV. Eights New Jerusalem.
Newton.   J.

Joseph made known to his brethren. Gen. xlv. 3. 4.

1 WHEN Joseph his brethren beheld
     Afflicted and trembling with fear
 His heart with compassion was fill'd,
     From weeping he could not forbear:
 A while his behaviour was rough;
     To bring their past sin to their mind
 But when they were humbled enough,
     He hasted to shew himself kind.

2 How little they thought it was he,
     Whom they had ill treated and sold!
 How great their confusion must be,
     As soon as his name he had told!
 " I am Joseph your brother, he said,
     And still to my heart you are dear,
                                    You

You sold me, and thought I was dead,
  But God for your sakes sent me here."

3 Tho' greatly distressed before,
  When charg'd with purloining the cup,
They now were confounded much more
  Not one of them durst to look up.
" Can Joseph, whom we would have slain
  Forgive us the evil we did?
And will he our housholds maintain!
  O this is a brother indeed"!

4 Thus dragg'd by my conscience I came,
  And laden with guilt, to the Lord:
Surrounded with terror and shame,
  Unable to utter a word.
At first he look'd stern and severe,
  What anguish then pierced my heart
Expecting each moment to hear,
  The sentence, " Thou cursed depart."

5 But oh! what surprise when he spoke,
  While tenderness beam'd in his face:
My heart then to pieces was broke
  O'erwhelm'd & confounded by grace
Poor sinner I know thee full well,
  By thee I was sold and was slain;

But

  But I dy'd to redeem thee from hell,
   And raise thee in glory to reign.

6 I am Jesus whom thou hast blasphem'd,
   And crucify'd often afresh;
  But let me henceforth be esteem'd,
   Thy brother, thy bone, and thy flesh
  My pardon I freely bestow,
   Thy wants I will fully supply;
  I'll guide thee and guard thee below,
   And soon will remove thee on high.

7 Go, publish to sinners around,
   That they may be willing to come,
  The mercy which now you have found
   And tell them that yet there is room.
  Oh, sinners, the message obey!
   No more vain excuses pretend;
  But come without further delay,
   To JESUS, our brother, and friend.

HYMN CCCXXV. The Coll. P. M. 8. of 8. *A.*

Longing after Christ.

1 I long to behold him array'd
   With glory and light from above;
  The King in his beauty display'd,
   His beauty of holiest love:

I languish and die to be there,
    Where Jesus hath fix'd his abode,
O when shall we meet in the air,
    And fly to the mountain of God.

2 With Him I on Zion shall stand,
    (For Jesus hath spoken the word)
The breadth of Immanuel's land
    Survey by the light of my LORD:
But when on thy bosom reclin'd,
    Thy face I am strengthened to see
My fulness of rapture I find,
    My Heaven of Heaven's in thee!

3 How happy the people that dwell
    Secure in the city above!
No pain the inhabitants feel,
    No sickness or sorrow shall prove:
Physician of souls unto me
    Forgiveness and holiness give,
And then from the body set free,
    And then to the city receive.

HYMN CCCXXVI.   The Coll.   A.
A Funeral Hymn.

1 AH! lovely appearance of death,
    No sight upon earth is so fair;

Not all the gay pageants that breathe,
   Can with a dead body compare;
With solemn delight I survey
   The corps when the spirit is fled,
In love with the beautiful clay,
   And longing to lie in its stead.

2 How blest is our brother bereft
   Of all that cou'd burden his mind;
How easy the soul that has left
   The wearisome body behind!
Of evil incapable thou,
   Whose relics with envy I see;
No longer in misery now,
   No longer a sinner like me.

3 This earth is affected no more
   With sickness or shaken with pain;
The war in the members is o'er,
   And never shall vex him again:
No anger hence forward or shame,
   Shall redden this innocent clay,
Extinct is the animal flame,
   And passion is vanish'd away.

4 This languishing head is at rest
   Its thinking and aching are o'er;

FUNERAL HYMN.

This quiet immoveable breast
   Is heav'd by affliction no more;
This heart is no longer the seat
   Of trouble and torturing pain
It ceases to flutter and beat,
   It never shall flutter again.

5 The lids he so seldom could close,
   By sorrow forbidden to sleep,
Seal'd up in eternal repose,
   Have strangely forgotten to weep:
The fountains can yield no supplies,
   These hollows from water are free;
The tears are all wip'd from these eyes
   And evil they never shall see.

6 To mourn and to suffer is mine,
   While bound in a prison I breathe;
And still for deliverance pine,
   And press to the issues of death;
What now with my tears I bedew
   O might I this moment become;
My spirit created anew,
   My flesh be consign'd to the tomb.

HYMN

HYMN CCCXXVII. Eight's of twice 3 syllables & 2

The Coll. J.

Funeral.

1 Hosannah to Jesus on high!
   Another has enter'd his rest;
Another has 'scap'd to the sky,
   And lodg'd in Immanuel's breast:
The soul of our brother is gone
   To heighten the triumph above;
Exalted to Jesus'throne!
   Exalted by Jesus'love!

2 How happy the angels that fall
   Transported at Jesus'name!
The saints, whom he soonest shall call,
   To share in the feast of the Lamb!
No longer imprison'd in clay,
   Who next from this dungeon shall
Who first shall be summon'd away? (fly?
   My merciful God!--- is it I?

3 O Jesus,- if this be thy will,
   That suddenly I should depart,
Thy council of mercy reveal,
   And whisper the call to my heart:
O give me a signal to know
   If soon thou would'st have me remove
                  And

And leave the dull body below,
  And fly to the regions of love.

HYMN CCCXXVIII. Six Eights. The Collection. *J.*
For the Spirit of Adoption.

1 FATHER (if thou my father art)
    Send forth the Spirit of thy son;
  Breathe him into my panting heart,
  And make me know as I am known,
  Make me thy conscious child, that I
  May Father Abba, Father cry!

2 O that the comforter would come,
  Nor visit as a transient guest;
  But fix in me his constant home,
  And keep possession of my breast,
  And make my soul his lov'd abode,
  The temple of the indwelling God!

3 Come Holy Ghost my soul inspire,
  Attest that I am born again;
  Come and baptize me, Lord, with fire,
  Nor let thy former gifts be vain:
  O grant the sense of sin forgiven,
  O grant the earnest of my Heaven.

4 O give the indisputable seal,
  That ascertains the kingdom mine!

That powerful stamp I long to feel,
The signature of love divine;
O shed it in my heart abroad,
Fulness of love, of Heav'n of God!

HYMN CCCXXIX. Six Eights. President Davis.

The Pardoning God.

1 GReat God of wonders all thy ways,
    Are matchless, Godlike and di-
But the fair glories of thy grace [vine;
    More Godlike and unrival'd shine,
Who is a pardoning God like thee?
Or who has grace so rich and free?

2 Crimes of such horror to forgive,
    Such guilty daring worms to spare,
This is thy grand prerogative,
    And none shall in the honor share.
    Who, &c.

3 Angels and men, resign your claim,
    To pity, mercy, love and grace;
These glories crown Jehovah's name,
    With an incomparable blaze.
    Who, &c.

4 In wonder lost with trembling joy,
    We take the pardon of our God,

Pardon for crimes of deepest dye,
 A pardon bought with Jesus' blood.
  Who, &c.

5 O may this strange, this matchless grace,
 This God like miracle of love,
Fill the wide earth with grateful praise,
 And all the Angelic Hosts above,
  Who is a pard'ning God like thee?
  Or who has grace so rich and free?

CCCXXX. P. M. 6 of 8. The Coll.

Joining the Church.   *A.*

WELcome, thou well belov'd of God,
 Thou heir of grace redeem'd by
  [blood;
Welcome with us thine hand to join,
As partner of our lot divine:
 Abundant blessings from above,
 Give him, we pray, thou God of love.

2 With us the pilgrim's state embrace;
We're trav'ling to a blissful place,
The new Jerusalem above,
The radiant throne, the seat, of love.
 The Holy Ghost that knows the way,
 Conduct thee on from day to day!

3 The

3 The staff of promise now receive,
Thy weary footsteps to relieve,
The chief support the trav'ler knows,
Leaning on which he forward goes.
   Thus if for rest thy spirits call,
   Leaning on which he cannot fall.

4 With peace, with ceaseless peace beshod,
The shoes of peace receive of God;
These keep from pain the pilgrim's feet,
And make the rugged way seem sweet.
   So Sion's paths shall ever prove,
   The paths of joy, and peace and love,

5 Thus onward move with upright pace;
Stedfast pursue the gospel race:
Fill'd with the power of truth divine,
Prove all the strength of Jesus thine.
   Commission'd angels soon shall come,
   And waft thee to thy wish'd for home.

CCCXXXI. P. M. 6 of 8. (Ps. clxiv.)   A.

Trusting in God.

1 I'LL praise my maker with my breath,
   And when my voice is lost in death
Praise shall employ my nobler pow'rs,
My days of praise shall ne'er be past,

While

  While life, and thought, and being
Or immortality endures.   [last.

Why should I make a man my trust?
 Princes may die, and turn to dust:
Vain is the help of flesh and blood;
 Their breath departs their pomp and
  pow'r,
And thoughts all vanish in an hour;
 Nor can they make their promise good.

Happy the man whose hopes rely,
 On Israel's God, he made the sky,
And earth and seas with all their train,
 His truth forever stands secure:
He saves the oppress'd he feeds the poor,
 And none shall find his promise vain,

He loves his Saints, he knows them well;
 But turns the wicked down to hell:
 Thy God O Zion ever reigns;
Let ev'ry tongue, let ev'ry age,
 In this exalted work engage;
Praise him in everlasting strains.

       CCCXXXII.

CCCXXXII. P. M. 6 of 8. (Pſ. xix)   *A.*

The Book of Nature.

1 GReat God the heav'ns well order'd frame,
Declares the glory of thy name;
There thy rich works of wonder ſhine,
A thouſand ſtarry beauties there,
A thouſand radiant marks appear,
Of boundleſs pow'r and ſkill divine.

2 From night to day, from day to night,
The dawning and the dying light,
Lectures of heav'nly wiſdom read;
With ſilent eloquence they raiſe,
Our thoughts to our creator's praiſe,
And neither ſound nor language need.

3 Yet their divine inſtructions run,
Far as the journeys of the ſun,
And ev'ry nation knows their voice;
The ſun, like ſome young bridegroom dreſt,
Breaks from the chambers of the eaſt,
Rolls round and makes the earth rejoice.

4 Where e'er he ſpreads his beams abroad,
He ſmiles, and ſpeaks his maker God:

All nature joins to shew thy praise,
Thus God in ev'ry creature shines;
Fair as the book of Nature's lines,
But fairer is the book of Grace.

CCCXXXIII. Six eights. Greenfield tune. (Pf. 96.) J.

1 LET all the earth their voices raise,
    To sing the choicest psalm of praise
To sing and bless Jehovah's name;
    His glory let the heathens know,
His wonders to the nations shew,
    And all his saving works proclaim.

2 The Heathens know thy glory, Lord;
    The wond'ring nations read thy word
The nations have Jehovah known:
    Our worship shall no more be paid
To Gods which mortal hands have made,
    Our maker is our God alone.

3 He fram'd the Globe, he built the sky,
    He made the shining worlds on high,
And reigns compleat in glory there
    His beams are majesty and light;
His beauties how divinely bright!
    His temple how divinely fair.

Come

THE LORD REIGNETH.

4 Come the great day, the glorious hour,
    When earth shall feel his saving pow'r,
And barb'rous nations fear his name:
    Then shall the race of men confess,
The beauty of his holiness,
    And in his courts his grace proclaim
~~praising God.~~

HYMN CCCXXXIV. Twice 10 and twice 11 The Coll *J*.
The Lord reigneth.

1 YE servants of God, your master proclaim;
And publish abroad his wonderful name;
The name all victorious of Jesus extol;
His Kingdom is glorious, and rules
    over all.

2 God ruleth on high, almighty to save;
    And still he is nigh his presence we have,
The great congregation his triumph
    shall sing
Ascribing salvation to Jesus our King.

3 Salvation to God, who sits on the throne;
    Let all cry aloud and honour the Son:
Our Jesus praises, the Angels proclaim,
Fall down on their faces,
And worship the Lamb.

4 Then let us adore,
   And give him his right;
   All glory and pow'r,
   And wisdom and might:
   All honour and blessing,
   With Angels above,
   And thanks never ceasing,
   And infinite love.

HYMN CCCXXXV Twice 10 & twice 11 The Coll. J.

For thine is the Kingdom.

1 YE souls that are weak,
    And helpless, and poor,
  Who know not to speak;
    Much less to do more;
  Lo! here's a foundation
    For comfort and peace
  In Christ is salvation;
    The Kingdom is his.

2 Then be not afraid,
    All power is given
  To Jesus our head,
    In earth and in Heav'n;
  Thro' him we shall conquer
    The mightiest foes;

Our Captain is ſtronger
  Than all that oppoſe.

His pow'r from above
  He'll kindly impart;
So free is his love,
  So tender his heart,
Redeem'd with his merit
  We're waſh'd in his blood;
Renew'd by his Spirit
  We've power with God.

Thy grace we adore,
  Director divine;
The kingdom and pow'r
  And glory are thine:
Preſerve us from running
  On rocks or on ſhelves;
From foes ſtrong and cunning,
  And moſt from ourſelves.

Reign o'er us as King,
  Accompliſh thy will;
And pow'rfully bring
  Us forth from all ill;
Till falling before thee
  We laud thy lov'd name,

Ascribing the glory
To God and the Lamb.

HYMN CCCXXXVI. Twice 10 & twice 11 The Coll. J.

The Burden'd Sinner.

1 AH! what can I do,
Or how be secure
If justice pursue,
What heart can endure?
When God speaks in Thunder,
And makes himself known,
The heart breaks asunder,
Tho' harder then stone?

2 With terror I read
My sins heavy score,
Their number exceeds
The sand on the shore
Guilt makes me unable
To stand or to flee;
So Cain murder'd Abel,
And trembled like me.

3 Each sin, like his blood,
With terrible cry
Calls loud upon God,
To strike from on high,
Nor can my repentance,

Extended

  Extended by fear
 Reverſe the juſt ſentence
  'Tis juſt tho' ſevere.

4 The caſe is too plain,
  I have my own choice,
 Again and again
  I ſlighted his voice,
His warnings neglected,
  His patience abuſ'd,
His goſpel rejected,
  His mercy refuſ'd.

5 And muſt I then go
  Forever to dwell
In miſ'ry and woe
  With devils in hell!
O where is the Saviour
  I ſcorn'd in time paſt?
His word in my favour
  Would ſave me at laſt.

6 Lord Jeſus! on thee
  I venter to call,
O look upon me
  The vileſt of all:
For whom didſt thou languiſh
  And bled on the tree?

O pity my anguish,
   And say, " twas for thee."

7 A cause such as mine
   Will honour thy pow'r,
All hell will repine
   All Heav'n will adore,
If in condemnation
   Strict justice takes place,
It shines in salvation,
   More glor'ous thro' grace.

HYMN CCCXXXVII. Twice 10 & twice 11 Rippon's Coll.   *J.*

Praising Christ.

1 OUR Saviour alone,
   The Lord let us bless,
Who reigns on his Throne,
   The Prince of our peace;
Who ever more saves us
   By shedding his blood;
All hail, Holy Jesus,
   Our Lord and our God!

2 We thankfully sing
   Thy glory and praise,
Thou merciful spring

Of pity and grace:
Thy kindness for ever
To men will we tell,
And say, our dear Saviour
Redeems us from hell.

3 Preserve us in love,
While here we abide:
O never remove
Thy presence nor hide.
Thy glorious salvation,
'Till each of us see
With joy the bles'd vision,
Completed in thee.

HYMN CCCXXXVIII. Twice 10 & twice 11 Newtown J.

The Lord will provide. Gen. xxii. v. 14.

1 THO' troubles assail and dangers affright,
Tho' friends should all fail, and foes all unite;
Yet one thing secures us, whatever betide,
The promise assures us, the Lord will provide.

2 The birds without barn and store-house are fed:

From

From them let us learn to trust for
   our bread :   (deny'd,
His saints what is fitting shall not be
So long as 'tis written, " the Lord will
   provide."

3 We all may, like ships, by tempest be tost,
   On perilous deeps, but can not be lost;
   Tho' satan enrages the wind and the tide;
   Yet scripture engages, the Lord will
      provide.

4 His call we obey, like Abraham of old,
   We know not the way, but faith makes
      us bold :   (sure guide,
   For tho' we are strangers, we have a
   And trust in all dangers, the Lord will
      provide.

5 When satan appears to stop up our path,
   And fills us with fears, we triumph by
      faith :   (try'd)
   He cannot take from us, (tho' oft he has
   The heart chearing promise, the Lord
      will provide.

6 He tells us we're weak our hope is in vain,
   The good that we seek, we ne're shall obtain
                                                But

REPENTANT SINNER.

But when such suggestions our graces
    have try'd,   (provide.
This answers all questions, the Lord will

No strength of our own, nor goodness
    we claim,
Our trust is all thrown on Jesus' name;
In this our strong tower for safety we hide
The Lord is our power, the Lord will
    provide.

When life sinks apace, and death is in
    view,   (us through;
The word of his grace shall comfort
Not fearing or doubting with Christ on
    our side,   (provide.
We hope to die shouting, the Lord will

HYMN CCCXXXIX. Twice 10, & twice. 11,
        Repentant sinner.   The Coll.   J.

DEAR Jesus, here comes,
    And knocks at thy door,
A beggar for crumbs,
    Distressed and poor:
Blind, lame, and forsaken,
    All roll'd in his blood,
At last overtaken,

                               When

REPENTANT SINNER.

When running from GOD.

2 To aſk children's bread,
   I dare not preſume,
But, LORD, to be fed,
   With fragments I come:
Some crumbs from thy table,
   O let me obtain,
For lo, thou art able,
   My wants to ſuſtain.

3 I own I deſerve,
   No favour to ſee,
So long I did ſwerve,
   And wander from thee;
'Till brought by affliction,
   My follies to mourn,
Now under conviction,
   To thee I return.

4 Great GOD, my deſert,
   Is nothing but death,
And hence to depart,
   For ever in wrath;
Yet, LORD to this city,
   Of refuge I flee,
O let thine eye pity,
   A ſinner like me!

5 For since thou hast said,
   Thou wilt cast out none,
That flee to thine aid,
   As sinners undone:
Now, LORD, I am come as,
   Condemned to die,
And on this sweet promise,
   I humbly rely.

6 I cannot depart,
   Dear JESUS, nor yield,
'Till feels my poor heart,
   This promise fulfill'd,
That I may for ever,
   A monument be,
To praise thee free Saviour,
   Of sinners like me.

CCCXL. Four 10, & twice 11. (Ps. l.) *J.*

The last Judgment.

The God of glory sends his summons forth
   Calls the south nation & awakes the north
From east to west the sov'reign orders spread,
'Thro' distant worlds & regions of the dead
The trumpet sounds; hell trembles: heav'n
      rejoices;
Lift up your heads, ye saints, with chear-
      ful voices.   2 No

THE LAST JUDGMENT.

2 No more shall Atheists mock his long delay:
His vengeance sleeps no more; behold the day;
Behold the judge descends, his guards are nigh;
Tempests and fire attend him down the sky.
When GOD appears, all nature shall adore him:
While sinners tremble, saints rejoice before him.

3 "Heav'n, earth, and hell, draw near; let all things come
" To hear my sentence and the sinners doom
" But gather first my saints; (the Judge commands)
" Bring them, ye angels, from their distant lands.
When Christ returns, wake ev'ry chearful passion;
And shout, ye saints, he comes for your salvation.

4 Behold my cov'nant stands for ever good
Seal'd by th' eternal sacrifice in blood,
And sign'd with all their names; the Greek, the Jew, That

That paid the ancient worship or the new.
There's no distinction here join all your voices
And raise your heads, ye saints, for heav'n rejoices.

5 " Here (saith the Lord) ye angels, spread their thrones,
' And near me seat my favourites and my (sons.
' Come, my redeem'd, possess the joys prepar'd,
' Ere time began ; 'tis your divine reward.
When Christ returns, wake ev'ry chearful passion ;
And shout, ye saints, he comes for your salvation.

HYMN CCCXLI. Elevens. Rippon's Coll. J.

Exceeding great and precious promises.

1 HOW firm a foundation ye saints of the LORD,
Is laid for your faith in his excellent word
What more can he say than to you he hath said?
You, who unto JESUS for refuge have fled

2 In ev'ry condition, in sickness, in health
In poverty's vale, or abounding in wealth;

At

"At home & abroad, on the land, on the sea
"As thy days may demand, shall thy
"strength ever be.

3 "Fear not, I am with thee, O be not
"dismay'd,
"I, am thy God, and will still give
"thee aid;
"I'll strengthen thee, help thee, and
"cause thee to stand,
"Upheld by my righteous omnipotent
"hand.

4 "When thro' the deep waters I call thee
"to go,
"The rivers of woe shall not thee over-
"flow;
"For I will be with thee, thy troubles
"to bless,
"And sanctify to thee, thy deepest dist-
"ress,

5 "When thro' fiery trials thy path-way
"shall lie,
"My grace all sufficient shall be thy supply
"The flame shall not hurt thee I only design
"Thy dross to consume, and thy gold to
"refine.

6 "Even

6 " Even down to old age, all my people
   " shall prove,
  " My sov'reign, eternal, unchangeable
   " love;
  " And when hoary hairs shall their
   " temples adorn,
  " Like lambs they shall still in my bo-
   " som be born.

7 " The soul that on Jesus hath lean'd for
   " repose,
  " I will not, I will not desert to his foes;
  " That soul tho' all hell should endea-
   " vour to shake,
  " I'll never--no never--no never forsake."

HYMN CCCXLII.   Lyric Poems.   J.

Judgment.

WHEN the fierce north wind with
    his airy forces
Rears up the Baltick to a foaming fury:
And the red lightning, with a storm of
    hail comes,
            Rushing amain down.
2 How the poor sailors stand amaz'd and
    tremble!
While the hoarse thunder, like a bloody
    trumpet,   Roar

Roar aloud onset to the gaping waters,
>> Quick to devour them.

3 Such shall the noise be, & the wild disorder
(If things eternal may be like these earthly)
Such the dire terror when the great arch-
angel,
>> Shakes the creation.

4 Tears the strong pillars of the vault of
Heaven,
Breaks up old marble, the repose of princes;
See the graves open, and the bones arising,
>> Flames all around 'em.

5 Hark, the shrill outcries of the guilty
wretches!
Lively bright horror, and amazing anguish
Stare thro' their eye-lids while the living
worm lies,
>> Gnawing within them.

6 Thoughts like old vultures, prey upon
their heart strings,
And the smart twinges, when the eye beholds the

Lofty

PERSEVERANCE.

Lofty judge frowning, and a flood of vengeance,
            Rolling afore him.

7 Hopeless immortals! how they scream
  and shiver,
While devils push them to the pit wide-
  yawning
Hideous and gloomy, to receive them
  headlong
            Down to the centre

8 Stop here my fancy, (all away ye horrid
Doleful Ideas,) come to Jesus,
How he sits God-like & the saints around
  him,
            Thron'd yet adoring

9 O may I sit there when he comes trium-
  phant,
Dooming the nations! then ascend to glory
While our Hosannas all along the passage,
            Shout the Redeemer.

HYMN CCCXLIII. P. M. Mrs. P———r A.
              Perseverance.

1 NOW Christ again to me appears
    Banishing all my doubts and fears
                                With

With his surprising grace;
He says fear not for you I died,
Remove thy doubts, look in my side,
Thy soul with joy at my right hand
   At the last day I'll place.

2 Tho' sin within thee yet remains
Against thy will it's grace that reigns,
And shall the conqu'ror prove;
Sin, earth and hell in vain combine,
To pluck thee from those hands of mine
Thou art secured in the arms
   Of everlasting ~~love~~.

3 Fear not tho' all the earth engage
Against thy soul, with hellish rage;
I'm earth's foundation's prop:
The government is laid on me,
I have all power to succour thee;
Then lean on my eternal arm
   I'll not deceive thy hope.

4 They sooner may the mountains move
Than thee destroy or change my love,
Or alter what I swore,
The Sun and Moon may cease to shine,
The Earth and all therein decline;

                      But

But my eternal love stands firm
And shall for evermore.

HYMN CCCXLIV. P. M. Mrs. P——r. *A.*
Faith looks within the vail.

WHEN I look up to Heaven,
And there my Jesus view;
When faith to me is given,
Those wonders to pursue:
I cry out O amazing,
Astonish'd at the sight;
And ever would be gazing,
In raptures of delight.

There on a throne most glorious,
With sweet delight I see,
Exalted and victorious,
The Man that died for me;
Co-equal and eternal,
He'll with the Father reign;
And all his foes infernal
Against him rage in vain.

He shines through Heav'ns glad regions
With such transcendant light,
All the celestial legions,
Are daz'led at the sight;

With faces veil'd before him,
Bright Cherubs lowly fall,
And joyfully adore him,
As Sovereign Lord of all.

4 The saints with joy and gladness,
Inveil'd before him stand,
Forever freed from sadness,
With victory in their hands;
In spotless robes adorned
Crowns on their heads they wear,
Tho' once by sinners scorned
Now like their Lord appear.

5 They join their greatful voices,
To praise the sacred Three,
All Heaven around rejoices,
In sweetest harmony;
To God the glorious Father,
The Spirit and the Son,
By all his works together,
Be equal honour done.

A.

ADORING Jesus, 260, 290.
Address to the Holy Spirit, 2.
Ascension of Christ, 51.
Attraction of the Cross, 77.
Almost Christian, 146.
All gracious God thy people bless, 152.
Awake and sing the song of Moses and the Lamb, 163.
Association of Churches, 204, 205, 207.
An happy moment, 303.

B.

BOOK of God's word and nature, 7, 48.
Blessing God, 15
Breathing after the Holy Spirit, 31.
Breathing after Holiness, 57.
Blessed Gospel, 60.
Believer's Hope, 91.
Breathing after Heavenly things, 93.
Baptism, 168, 170, 171, 172, 173, 174, 175, 274.
Bleeding Saviour, 193.
Blessings of the Gospel, 262.
Barren Fig-Tree, 266.
Backslider's Prayer, 279, 280.
Birth of Christ, 286.
Buried with Christ in Baptism, 302.
Book of Nature, 332.
Burdened Sinner, 336.

C.

CRAVING the Spirit, 18.
Creation and Providence, 27.
Clean Heart, 29.
Condescension of God, 40.
Creation and Redemption, 42.
Christ and His Church, 50.
Christ precious, 58.
Christ's Intercession, 63.
Contrition, 78.
Christian Soldier, 81.

Christian's

INDEX.

Christian's Expectation, 92.
Complaint of Spiritual Sloth, 112.
Christian happy, 121.
Chusing the better part, 129.
Confidence, 136.
Completeness of Christ, 137.
Christ the only Saviour, 140.
Christ Justifies and Sanctifies, 159.
Christ's Kingdom and Majesty, 164.
Complaint of Ingratitude, 166.
Commission, 169.
Constitution of a Church, 194, 195, 196, 197.
Covenant God, 264.
Ceremonial Law, 268.
Christ's Resurrection, 276.
Christ our Life, 283.
Converse with Christ, 298.
Christ the believer's All, 301.
Come thou font of every blessing, 304.
Come, descend, O heavenly Spirit, 305.
Christ withdrawn, 322.

D.

DELIGHT in Public Worship, 21.
Devout Retirement, 53.
Dismission, 68, 69, 151, 161, 166, 313.
Desiring assurance of God's favour, 74.
Different Success of the Gospel, 113.
Deadness under the word, 115.
Dying Saviour, 127, 181.
Desiring the Divine Presence, 135.
Distress of Soul, 157.
Divine Glories and Graces, 180.
Doubting, 285.
Death and Glory, 306.

E.

EXHORTING to Worship, 19.
Exhortation to Praise, 24.
Excellency of the Scriptures, 28.
Encouragement to wait on God, 54.

Ezekiel xxxvi. 26. 107.
Exceeding great and precious promises, 341.

F.

FEAR not, 38.
Flesh and Spirit, 116.
Faith in Christ our Sacrifice, 162.
Fasts and Thanksgiving for Victory, 208, 209, 210, 211, 213.
Fasts and Thanksgiving, 219.
Funeral, 220, 221, 222, 223, 224, 226, 227, 228, 229, 230, 231, 232, 233, 234, 326, 327.
Funeral Thought, 225.
Family Worship, 235, 237, 238, 239, 240, 241, 242, 243, 244, 245, 246, 247, 248, 249, 250, 251, 252, 253, 254, 255, 256, 257, 258, 259.
Finished Redemption, 295, 314.
Faith's Claim, 261.
For thine is the Kingdom, 335.
For the Spirit of adoption. 338.
Faith looks within the vail, 344.

G.

GOD glorified in the Gospel, 8.
Gospel worthy of all-acceptance, 32.
Goodness of God, 33.
God's presence in his house, 37.
Glorious Gospel, 39.
God exalted above all praise, 43.
Gospel Jubilee, 46.
God's Reasoning with men, 55.
Grace, 61, 160.
God our only Happiness, 73.
General, 82.
Godly Sorrow for Christ's Sufferings, 83.
Glory and Grace in the Person of Christ, 134.
God's promise unchangeable, 142.
God our Support, 269.
Gospel Trumpet, 275.

H.

HEAVENLY Worship, 10.
Holy Boldness, 11, 97.

Heavenly Joy on Earth, 23.
Heavenly Praise, 25.
Holy Walk, 52.
Hell the Sinner's own place, 67.
How Sad our State by Nature is, 101.
Heavenly Guest, 108.
Heart devoted to God, 141.
Holy Ghost, 155.
Heavenly Journey, 287.

I.

INVOKING the Spirit, 1, 22.
Invitation, 5, 98, 145, 312, 315.
Invitation of Christ, 17.
Joys of Heaven, 30.
Immutability of God, 45.
Joyful Courſe, 56.
Jeſu, Jeſu, deareſt Lord, 86.
Joy of Converſion, 105
Juſtification by Chriſt only, 117.
Inconſtancy, 156.
Iſaiah, 9, 2.
Jeſus Chriſt. 300.
Judgment, 308, 309, 310, 311, 321, 342.
Joſeph made known to his brethren, 324.
Joining the Church, 330.

K.

KINGDOM of God not in Word, but in power, 65.
Kingdom of Chriſt, 110.

L.

LORD's Day Morning, 3.
Loving kindneſs of God, 16.
Looking upwards, 34.
Longing after God, 41.
Lord is God, 47.
Lord I would ſpread my ſore diſtreſs, 104.
Living and dead Faith, 106.
Law and Goſpel, 144.
Love to God, 130.
Love of Chriſt ſhed abroad in the Heart, 150.

Lord's

INDEX.

Lord's Supper, 176, 177, 178, 183, 184, 185, 187, 188, 189, 190, 191, 192.
Longing after Christ, 325.
Let all the earth their voices raise, 333.
Lord reigneth, 334.
Lord will provide, 338.
Last Judgment, 340.

M.

MERCY and truth, 126.
Misimprovement of time, 133.
Mysteries of Providence, 153.
Meeting, 206.
Majesty of Christ, 272.
Morning and Evening, 293, 294.

N.

NEW Year's Day, 76, 265, 291.
Naked as from the earth we came, 96.

O.

OBEDIENCE and Death of Christ, 36.
Once more before we part, 165.
Ordination, 198, 199, 200, 201, 202, 203.
Opening Worship, 263.
Opening a Place of Worship, 273.

P.

PRAISE to God for Creation and Redemption, 9.
Public Prayer and Praise, 12.
Prayer, 14, 100, 154, 283.
Praise to our Creator, 20.
Providence and Grace, 49.
Preached Word, 59.
Pardoning Grace, 62.
Prospect of Heaven makes death easy, 70.
Praise to the Lamb, 72, 88.
Providence, 79.
Parable of the Sower, 85.
Pressure of Sin, 103.
Prayer and Hope, 111.
Perseverance, 118, 343.

Petition,

Petition, 120.
Preparing for Death, 123.
Pardon and Rest for the weary soul, 128, 132.
Passion and exaltation of Christ, 158.
Pardon and strength from Christ, 179.
Praise for National Peace, 112.
Public Fast, 214, 215, 216.
Power and Grace, 270.
Praise to God from all creatures, 271, 292.
Poor Sinner, 277, 278.
Pilgrim's Song, 282.
Prayer for revival, 316.
Praise to the Redeemer, 318.
Pardoning God, 329.
Praising Christ, 337.

R.

REVERENTIAL Worship, 4.
Resurrection of Christ, 64. 307
Rapture, 80.
Rejoicing in Hope, 87.
Renewing Grace, 102
Repentance, 119.
Remembering our latter end, 149.
Receiving a member, 186.
Rejoice, 267.
Redeeming Love, 289.
Relative Duties, 319.
Repentant Sinner, 339.

S.

SABBATH, 13.
Song to creating Wisdom, 26.
Spirituality of God, 44.
Successful Resolve, 66.
Sanctification sought, 71.
Safety in God, 75.
Salvation approaching, 84.
Sinner converted, 90. 297
Sympathising Saviour, 114.
Sense of Pardon desired, 122.
Saints dwell in Heaven, 131.

Sinner's Prayer, 138.
Stony Heart, 147.
Satan repulsed, 148.
Spirit, water and blood, 182.
Spiritual Barrenness, 296.
Seriousness, 297.
Spirit of Adoption, 328.

T.

TRIUMPHS of Grace, 6.
Thankfullness for Mercies, 35.
Tribulation, 94.
Trials overcome by Hope, 95.
Trust in God under difficulties, 139, 331.
True Penitence, 147.
Thanksgiving for victory, 213.
Thanksgiving, (Public) 217, 218.
True experience, 281.

V.

VOICE of Christ, 284.

W.

WATCHFULNESS and Prayer, 89.
Way and end, righteous and wicked, 99.
Weakness bewailed, 109.
Way to Canaan, 143
Word of God more precious than gold, 317.
Who hath our report believed, 320.
What think ye of Christ, 323.

A TABLE.

TABLE OF SCRIPTURES.

Book.	Chap.	Ver.	Hymn.
Genesis,	22,	14,	338
	45,	3, 4,	324
1 Samuel,	7,	12,	304
1 Kings,	18,	20—39,	47
2 Kings,	7,	4,	66
Esther,	4,	16,	66
Psalms,	73,	25,	73
	85,	15,	46
	115,	1,	72
Isaiah,	1,	18,	55
	9,	2,	299
	55,	1, &c.	98
Ezekiel,	36,	26,	107
Amos,	3,	1—6,	209
Zachariah,	13,	1,	101
Matthew,	11,	28,	17
	13,	3 & 10,	85
	22,	42,	323
	26,	41,	89
	28,	19,	169
John,	6,	65,	177
	12,	32,	77
	19,	24,	159
Acts,	1,	25,	67
	14,	22,	94
Romans,	6,	4,	302
Ephesians,	2,	5,	160
Philippians,	4,	4,	267
1 Timothy,	1,	11,	39
1 Timothy,	4,	8,	91
Hebrews,	6,	17—19,	142
	13,	20,	71
1 John,	5,	6,	180
Revelations,	3,	20,	128

FINIS.

www.ingramcontent.com/pod-product-compliance
Lightning Source LLC
Chambersburg PA
CBHW032020220426
43664CB00006B/315